GOOD BIRDERS
DON'T WEAR WHITE

GOOD BIRDERS
DON'T WEAR WHITE

50 Tips from
North America's Top Birders

Foreword by **PETE DUNNE**

Illustrations by **ROBERT A. BRAUNFIELD**

Edited by **LISA WHITE**

HOUGHTON MIFFLIN COMPANY
BOSTON · NEW YORK · 2007

Visit our Web site: www.houghtonmifflinbooks.com.

Library of Congress Cataloging-in-Publication Data

Good birders don't wear white : 50 tips from North
America's top birders.
p.   cm.
Includes bibliographical references.
ISBN-13: 978-0-618-75642-1
ISBN-10: 0-618-75642-6
1. Bird watching. I. Houghton Mifflin Company.
QL677.5.G64 2007
598.072'34 — dc22
2006030503

Book design by Dede Cummings & Carolyn Kasper / DCDESIGN

Printed in the United States of America

HAD 10 9 8 7 6 5 4 3 2 1

CONTENTS

Contents

Contents

The Road Less Traveled

List Lust

Cheer-up, Cheerily

Contents

Mind Your Manners

Feather Forecasting

Building a Nest Egg

Contents

Capturing the Moment

The Joy of Birding

Contents

Look! Up in the Sky!

Developing a Bird Brain

FOREWORD

I FIND MYSELF IN A VERY uncomfortable position here
— and I don't mean facing a computer screen with fingers dancing over the keyboard. Fact is, I write a lot —
books, articles, columns, you name it. If the topic relates directly or tacitly to birds, chances are I've dabbled in it. No,
my discomfort has nothing to do with any unfamiliarity. It
has to do with direction.

Almost always, when I sit down to write, I know precisely what I'm going to say and pretty much how I'm
going to say it. This time I'm at a loss. I know what I'm
supposed to do, and that is warm up readers for the great
act to follow. But that is also the problem. How can any one
writer hope to introduce a birding audience to the greatest
compilation of birding know-how of all time?

Okay, let's start with what this foreword is not going to
do. It is not going to beguile you with the hints, tricks,
shortcuts, and advice that expert birders bring to bear.
That is what the fifty contributors to this book have done:

synthesize more than a hundred years of birding tradition and approximately twenty-five hundred cumulative years of birding experience.

Who's going to try to compete with that?

This foreword is also not going to fall back on the old tried-and-true distraction employed by many writers in my position, which is to expound on my own experiences with birds, birding, and bird study.

Look. I've written whole books filled with anecdotal bird stuff like that. You passed them by in order to buy this one (and I can't gainsay your choice).

But in searching for an angle, I do find that I have an insider's insight that may pique a reader's interest. It turns out that I know virtually all of the contributors to these pages, recognizing all as colleagues and knowing many as friends. Many writers have an aversion to speaking about themselves, so with the authority vested in me, I think it might be fun to offer readers a peek behind the writer's mask and direct a descriptive word or two toward the contributing authors of *Good Birders Don't Wear White*.

Jon Dunn is a noted author and tour leader for WINGS and has been for many years the final word when it comes to tricky identifications. All photos of unidentified gulls and *Empidonax* flycatchers with borderline traits ultimately find their way into Jon's hands. Jon is affable and serious, intellectually gifted, and boasts an array of interests (we share a passion for American history). Tens of thousands of birders are better birders because of Jon and his teaching skill. If you are not counted among them, you soon will be.

Jessie Barry, at the tender age of thirteen, was a poster child for the American Birding Association. She and I appeared together in their membership brochure. The photo showed me pointing out a bird, Jessie looking on. I've always wanted to know what happened to the other hundred photos taken that day — the ones that showed Jessie pointing out birds to me. As memory serves, they were more representative of our day. Now that she is at the University of Washington, working on a degree in ecology and evolutionary biology and in her spare time on a field guide to North American waterfowl, Jessie's signature expression is "Uhmmmm." When she starts humming this mantra, it means her binoculars are fused to something really good *andyoubettergetonitFAST*.

The last time I heard it, she was looking at a Summer Tanager from the porch of the person who claims the largest yard list in North America. The bird proved to be number 307 for Paul Lehman, a Cape May resident celebrated for his knowledge of bird distribution. Open almost any field guide. If Paul didn't actually draft the range maps, he was almost certainly consulted. His hobby is finding new bird species for North America. His happy hunting ground is the Inuit village of Gambel on St. Lawrence Island. I don't know whether Paul has actually been adopted by the tribe, but he is on the tribal leader's e-mail birthday greeting list.

Paul's yard list total now? Just hit 314. Magnificent Frigatebird. As fortune had it, he was away from home last week, when the Gray Kingbird perched on the utility lines just down the street from his porch. Yep, you guessed it, Paul was on Gambel.

When it comes to just plain enjoying birds, few can stand on the same platform with Victor Emanuel, founder and director of Victor Emanuel Nature Tours. Victor's signature expression is "Wow." Search the world over, and you'll find nothing that beats "Wow." But what distinguishes Victor is not so much the expression as the lavishness with which it is applied. Victor says "Wow" about almost any bird. A White-eyed Vireo in full view garners a "Wow." A Northern Cardinal in sunlight earns a "Wow." A Painted Redstart, dancing through the oaks in Cave Creek Canyon (where Victor and I used to co-lead his youth birding camps) is always sanctified with a "Wow." Often several.

And you know, no matter how many vireos or cardinals you've seen (and I've seen hundreds), when Victor says

"Wow," by golly, you get that sense of wow, too. Wow is infectious. Victor the vector.

I can't begin to express how delighted I was to see John Kricher's name ranked among the authors. I met John, a college professor and ecologist, in the summer of 1977. He was teaching a marsh ecology course; I was struggling to give standing and solvency to an institution called the Cape May Bird Observatory.

Not long ago I was working on a book project that involved reading virtually all of the 716 volumes that constitute *The Birds of North America*. This comprehensive ornithological work was designed to impart the sum of knowledge relating to North American birds and, as such, was never intended to make for light reading. But the intent didn't necessarily preclude this possibility, and while reading the account for Black-and-white Warbler, I was surprised by the entertaining and readable quality of the piece. I turned to the cover to see who the author was, and you guessed it — John's name was there. Scientist and wordsmith — two great but by no means singular qualities.

This book will introduce you to other contributors who are both able scientists and capable communicators — Paul Kerlinger, author and bird migration expert who did his seminal work on migrating raptors by using an old police radar in Cape May, and David Bird, McGill University professor and radio show host.

It's a slippery slope I've placed myself on, realizing now that by singling out just some of the wonderful and talented contributors to this book, I will inevitably fail to do justice to them all.

It would be unthinkable not to draw the reader's attention to Bill Thompson III, editor of *Bird Watcher's Digest* and author of *Bird Watching for Dummies;* Amy Hooper, editor of *WildBird;* and Chuck Hagner, editor in chief of *Birder's World*. The talent they bring to their respective magazines is reflected here, too.

Popular bird magazines are as visually arresting as the birds that are their subject. So in these pages you'll find contributions from celebrated photographers such as Richard Crossley and Kevin Karlson (coauthors of the new shorebird guide), Arthur Morris and Tim Gallagher.

Tim Gallagher . . . Tim Gallagher . . . now where (you are thinking) *have I heard that name before?*

Well, if you subscribe to *Living Bird,* you may recognize him as the magazine's editor in chief. But unless you've been living in a cave in Tibet, I'll bet you heard his name associated with the rediscovery of the Ivory-billed Woodpecker.

Oh, that Tim Gallagher. Precisely.

The slate of writers is just as stellar as the cast of photographers and includes well-known names such as Don and Lillian Stokes (birding's "First Couple"), Scott Shalaway (Mr. Backyard Birder himself), the incomparable (and unsinkable) Judith Toups and, of course, Scott Weidensaul.

You know, Scott, Roger Peterson once said that if he could paint like anyone else, it would be Robert Bateman. I just want to go on record saying that if I could write like anyone else, it would be Scott Weidensaul.

And readers are probably thinking, Well, if he's less verbose than you are, Dunne, I wish you wrote like Scott, too.

You're right. I'm running out of space. You're running out of patience. The only things I'm not running out of are talented personalities to commend to you.

Scott, you're a writer. How do I get out of the jam I'm in? Time for a deus ex machina? My deus, I almost forgot to mention Kenn Kaufman and David Sibley, whose celebrated names grace the spines of two of the dog-eared field guides you most certainly own. And Peter Alden (a guy who was leading bird tours for Massachusetts Audubon to places such as Africa back when birders considered a trip to the Everglades foreign travel) and Wayne Petersen (who leads them now). And Peter Stangel and Paul Baicich, two of the conservation cornerstones of birding. And Louise Zemaitis and Julie Zickefoose. Louise and Julie have a great deal in common. In addition to being wonderful people (and having last names that begin with Z), both are superlative artists.

From not knowing where to go with this foreword, I find that I have written myself into a real corner. Hit my word limit and still have a lot of names to flag. When writers get in a jam like this, they inevitably turn to their editors, and this foreword has finally inclined to her. Lisa White, a wonderful person and a credit to her profession. No one else in North America could have engaged the talents of the many experts housed in this book.

Kudos to you, Lisa. Hats off to them.

You're curious about the title of the book? Ah, well, now you strike close to the heart of the matter (and very close to my own heart as well). The title comes from one of the essays found here — an essay written by Sheri Williamson of Southeastern Arizona Bird Observatory (and author of the *Peterson Field Guide to Hummingbirds of North America*). This essay was first published in my book *Pete Dunne on Bird Watching*. It garnered Lisa White's attention and triggered this book.

And so now, finally, you come to know how it came to be that out of all these talented and well-known birding personalities, I was the one chosen to write the foreword.

Professional courtesy. Right of first refusal. Had the essay first. But what really counts is who has it last.

That is you. So start turning pages and savoring the wit and wisdom of *Good Birders Don't Wear White*.

— PETE DUNNE
Vice President, Natural History Information
New Jersey Audubon Society's Cape May Bird Observatory

Come On-a My House

1. Relinquish Control for Stress-free Bird Feeding
by Mike O'Connor

WHAT DO YOU THINK ABOUT this statement? "A backyard bird feeder will help take the stress out of your life." A friend of mine uses that line to promote her birding shop in Barnegat, New Jersey. It's warm, appealing, and will, with luck, help her turn a lot of people on to birding. However, with no offense to my friend, stress-free bird feeding falls into the same category as painless dentistry. It just doesn't happen. In fact, I can't think of a hobby that causes more stress than bird feeding.

Of course, bird feeding shouldn't be stressful. It should simply be an act of putting out a bit of food and enjoying whatever comes. But this is America, damn it! We must decide who eats and when, and we won't relax until everything goes our way.

That last line isn't meant to be a political statement (unless you thought it was and liked it); it is meant to show that most of us feel the need to control everything we can, even something as simple as feeding birds. Let's take Ted, for example. (Ted is not a real person. It's just an easy name for me to spell.) Ted, for whatever reason, decides today is the day that he's going to start feeding birds, so Ted goes out and buys himself a thistle feeder. After a few skinned knuckles, he assembles the feeder, which is the complicated task of sliding three perches into a tube. Next he fills it with thistle. He then makes a mental note, as he sweeps piles of seed from the kitchen floor, to fill the feeder outside next time. After hanging the feeder in front of the kitchen window (where all feeders are required by law to be hung), he goes to bed dreaming of birds eating from his new feeder.

In the morning, Ted awakens to find that a true miracle has happened. There are indeed birds at his new feeder. Not just any birds either, we are talking handsome American Goldfinches, and not just one or two but a dozen or more! The excited Ted calls everyone he knows, and all of his friends rush over to see Ted's goldfinches. Ted is the man of the hour, and it's all thanks to his new feeder. So, you ask, what's so bad about that? You'll see.

Eventually, new birds arrive at his feeder. (Ah, the thot plickens.) These new birds are also attractive. The book says they are House Finches. Wow, with only one feeder, Ted has attracted two species of birds. Good, right? Well, you might think so, but Ted notices that while the House Finches are chowing down, those cuter and much shyer goldfinches are waiting in the tree, afraid to come to the feeder. One of Ted's friends says, "Hey, what happened to the nice goldfinches?" Suddenly Ted feels his position as man of the hour slipping away. He runs outside, waving his arms like a man possessed, causing the House Finches to fly off, thus allowing the goldfinches to return. Success! But only for a moment. Once the House Finches realize that Ted is not a threat but merely another control freak, they quickly return. Ted then races back outside to chase the interlopers away. From that point on, Ted has unknowingly entered the dark side of bird feeding.

Every day for the past twenty-five years I have dealt with people just like Ted. They are nice people who want to enjoy nature, but they also have a preconceived idea about which birds will be at their feeders. Yes, a bird feeder will attract goldfinches and cardinals, but a feeder will also attract creatures that aren't featured on the pretty package of birdseed. Crows, jays, grackles, and blackbirds put otherwise calm people over the edge by doing nothing more than taking something that is being offered. People (and you know who you are) bang on the window, yell through the screen, and complain bitterly to me that "the good birds are being chased away by the big birds!"

This is only the beginning. I have yet to mention the *S* word. The one creature that will make the most sedate person's neck veins bulge. One day I waited on a grown woman who had just been treated for a broken arm. Why? Not because she fell while skiing or because she was hurt while trying to stop a bank robbery. This woman broke her arm when she fell chasing a squirrel across her backyard. I am not kidding. Wouldn't you love to have heard her explaining that to the people in the emergency room?

You know, folks, it doesn't have to be this way. The best feeder I've ever seen is one that you can't buy. This feeder is at the Cape Cod Museum of Natural History. It is nothing more than a twelve-foot horizontal log with little pockets that someone hacked out to hold birdseed. Throughout the day, a treasury of wildlife visits this wonderful log feeder. Jays, chickadees, juncos, sparrows, cardinals, crows, chipmunks, skunks, raccoons, and yes, even the *S*-word creatures all come and eat from this log. And they all eat in peace. There is no screwball banging on the glass or psycho chasing after them with a stick.

A simple log feeder, or any feeder for that matter, could indeed take the stress out of our lives, if only we could observe and appreciate nature and not try to control it. This suggestion is probably way too late for you people who are already feeding birds. More than likely you joined the dark side of bird feeding long ago. But for anyone out there who is thinking about feeding birds for the first time, it's not too late. Put out your feeder and enjoy what happens. Forget about having to control everything. The creatures will work it out themselves. Save your controlling needs for something in life that really matters. I'm talking about the remote control for the TV. You never want to give that up.

———

MIKE O'CONNOR opened the Bird Watcher's General Store in Orleans, Massachusetts, in 1983. He writes a weekly birding column called "Ask the Bird Folks" for *The Cape Codder* and has recently written the book *Why Woodpeckers Don't Get Headaches: And Other Answers to Bird Questions You Know You Want to Ask*.

2. *Turn Your Backyard into a Wildlife Sanctuary*
by Connie Toops

I T WAS SPRING OF 1970, my freshman year at Ohio State University. The scene: a guy in zoology class asks me to go bird watching. He'll pick me up Saturday, and we'll head south of Columbus to study migrants for his Ornithology 401 midterm.

Pat arrives in a ragtag Rambler station wagon. It chugs to a state park, and we select a narrow, wooded trail. I carry no-name binoculars I obtained by redeeming S & H Green Stamps. Monstrous 20 × 50s adorn his chest. We walk for a few minutes, then he points and whispers, "Rose-breasted Grosbeak."

My birding experience is limited to wrens, woodpeckers, and cardinals. Who's this bozo kidding with a name like Rose-breasted Grosbeak? I aim my glasses in the general direction but have no idea what to expect.

"Do you see it?" he inquires.

"No."

"Up there," he murmurs, slipping behind and encircling me with his arms as he lowers the 20 × 50s to my eyes. Highly magnified branches wiggle wildly. The more I try to focus, the dizzier I become. I realize a man I do not know has his arms around me on a remote trail. I don't want to scream, so I lie.

"I see it."

"Really?" he says suspiciously. "It flew."

Luckily, it perches on a bare branch. When I finally focus on the elusive black-and-white bird with crimson ascot, I gasp. Awed by the moment, I have no inkling that I will share more than thirty-five years of birding adventures with the man beside me, or that we will eventually attract these breathtaking birds to our yard.

During the three subsequent decades, Pat and I have learned much about transforming backyards into birding hot spots. We improved yards in Mississippi, West Virginia, and Maryland for a wealth of species, including bluebirds, hummingbirds, towhees, and titmice.

Enhancing backyard habitat has become tremendously popular with urban and suburban dwellers, who can convert a barren lawn into an oasis for wildlife by sprinkling a water feature here or adding plants there to provide food, shelter, and nesting cover. Here are a few tips on how to do it.

TIP 1: DIVERSITY MATTERS

In western North Carolina, we discovered a languishing mountainside farm, ripe in diversity, with fruit trees, pasture, brushy fencerows, thickets, hardwood forest, and clear-running streams. To that nurturing mix, we added native meadow in lieu of lawn — beds of nectar-bearing flowers to please hummingbirds and butterflies, fruit-laden trees and shrubs, and an array of nest boxes sized for everything from wrens to owls. As biologists, we know that the more diverse our property is, the more wildlife it will attract.

Rose-breasted Grosbeaks are generalists in food and habitat requirements, much like their cardinal cousins. Massive beaks allow them to crush and devour wild grapes, cherries, blackberries, dogwood fruits, and weed seeds. While nesting, they consume countless creeping and hopping insects, including tent and gypsy moth caterpillars, cankerworms, even potato beetles. Suburban yards, especially those shaded by maple, oak, or basswood trees, provide perfect places to balance their twiggy nests on forked limbs.

Not all of our avian guests are as easy to please. Eastern Bluebirds are passionate about our pasture, returning earlier than other spring migrants to claim choice tree cavities or nest boxes near the grassy fields on our farm. Like grosbeaks, bluebirds switch from winter fruits to a high-protein diet of insects while raising young. Their best hunting occurs in mowed grass rather than fields rank with weeds and grasses. Suburban birders are often very successful when offering nest boxes to bluebirds because mowed lawns (if the neighborhood is not drenched with lawn-care chemicals) are perfect sources of crickets, beetles, and spiders.

On our mountainside, bluebirds choose a favorite box in the south-facing pasture, where insects are prevalent in April and May. When waist-high grasses obscure insect quarry in summer, the bluebirds relocate to a regularly mowed area near our garden for their second brood. Why don't we cut the pasture? We also host Golden-winged Warblers, whose numbers are plummeting because of habitat loss. These lovely birds, recognized by golden foreheads and gold wing patches, inhabit old fields that are becoming thickets. They nest at the base of sturdy plants such as goldenrod and hunt for spiders, moths, and caterpillars hidden among the leaves of young locusts, dogwoods, and viburnum shrubs. We manage for Golden-winged Warblers by allowing alternating portions of the pasture to mature for a decade, then clearing them and beginning anew.

TIP 2: PLANT WILDLIFE MAGNETS

Most people who enhance backyards for birds do so in the hope of attracting a beloved species. Neighbors in West Virginia were enamored of goldfinches and began their quest to host them by hanging nyjer seed feeders near the patio. Later they planted purple coneflowers and black-eyed Susans — natives with seasonal seeds that gold-finches relish. Another friend wanted hummingbirds in her yard, so she planted a spring-through-autumn progression of perennials — wild columbine, coral-bells, bee balm, jewelweed, and cardinal flower — to supply the nectar-filled red flowers hummers thrive on.

No matter where you live, you can enhance the surrounding habitat with fruit-, seed-, nectar-, or shelter-producing plants that act as magnets to entice target birds to your doorstep. All it takes is a bit of research in birding magazines and gardening catalogs or on the Internet to match the species you desire with plants, nest boxes, or water features that will lure them.

TIP 3: ENJOY THE VIEW

Adding key plants, growing sheltering trees and shrubs, or installing water features takes more than a weekend. Enhancing your backyard to lure new birds becomes a lifestyle. Before you undertake this effort, look around to decide where the investment makes most sense — perhaps near the patio or outside a dining room window. Then train yourself in another important behavior: pause often to enjoy the view!

Through the years, Pat and I have developed an unspoken rule. Whenever we catch the first spring glimpse

of black, white, and rose at our feeder, we grab our binoculars and relive the moment we saw the bird that changed
our lives.

––––––––––––

The freelance nature writer and photographer CONNIE
TOOPS lives on a 128-acre mountainside farm in western
North Carolina (www.lostcovefarm.com). She has written
numerous books and magazine articles and travels widely
to speak on birding, wildlife gardening, and nature photography subjects.

3. *Open a Restaurant: A Maître d' for the Birds*
by David M. Bird

THE TABLES ARE SET and I await my feathered guests. I call it Dave's Bird Bistro. I smile smugly at the clever play I have made on my name as I stand near the back window gazing at my bird feeders hanging from the pole in the early dawn. No reservations accepted, and first come, first served!

As someone who has been in the "bird buffet" business for years, I figure that I've got all the bases covered for my clients: several basic feeders and plenty of water nearby for drinking and washing up. A little something for everybody.

Ah, here come my first guests, right on cue. Cardinal Richelieu accompanied by his lover alight on the hanging platform feeder. Since they forgo the arduous fall migration, Northern Cardinals are year-round customers. They are also among my fussiest guests and arguably the most sought after in North American backyards. Being a tad shy, they prefer a table away from my window and usually show up only just after dawn and right before dusk. Watching the bright scarlet male tenderly place a tidbit into the beak of the often underappreciated tan and red female could thaw the hearts of the starchiest of maître d's.

As strikingly beautiful as they are, cardinals are not my favorite feeder birds. That honor falls to the rather handsome Dark-eyed Juncos. Looking like bank executives in their gray and white garb, they seldom land on my feeders, surprisingly preferring the indignity of rummaging through the table scraps spilled on the ground below the feeders.

Throughout the day, cocky little Black-capped Chickadees flit back and forth like high-energy teenagers, turning my bistro into nothing more than a fast-food operation. Quickly grabbing sunflower seeds from my tube feeder, they dash off to some nearby cover, either to crack them open for the tasty treat within or to stuff them into crevices for another day. On occasion, they'll cling to my suet cage and reach in to neatly gobble down some of the pure white fat. My bistro offers the commercially available rendered suet that does not easily melt in the warm sun. Because I am a conscientious maître d' who desires return guests, it is not in my best interests to offer greasy dishes that can potentially ruin their feathered apparel, which is critical to their survival. Certainly, getting grease all over their heads while feeding on melted suet is not healthy!

At any time of day, I can expect my suet feeder to bring in other beloved clientele — the Downy and Hairy Woodpeckers. For the most part, these elegant black-and-white celebrities do not mind being stared at, even at close range. Also attracted by the suet are the nuthatches, my wife's cherished friends. We are amused to watch these roundish, little birds with their snooty, upturned beaks sift through our sunflower seeds, as if they were shoppers feeling tomatoes at a vegetable stand, to find just the right one by its heft.

No classy bird restaurant would be complete without a tube feeder filled with nyjer seed, commonly referred to as thistle seed. Yes, it's the most expensive item on the menu, but depending on the time of year, I have been known to offer more than one tube at a time. Because American Goldfinches and House Finches adore nyjer seed and often bring along the whole neighborhood to dine on these revolving "tables," they are quickly emptied.

Sometimes I offer daily specials at my restaurant. As an experienced maître d', I can safely tell you that there is no better way to bring in the local Blue Jays than by laying out a couple of handfuls of unshelled peanuts. To my constant amazement, these cleverest of birds seem consistently to discover this treat within about five minutes of its being offered. Like the chickadees, they do not stay long. But one thing is for sure — they will keep returning to the table until every last one of those peanuts is gone!

Over the years of running my bistro, I have also worked hard to attract those very tiny customers, the ones that favor a liquid lunch. Yes, I'm referring to the hummingbirds. Even though I offer the finest of nectars from my cellar, the Ruby-throated Hummingbird graces my red-trimmed glass feeder only on an occasional basis in the summer.

While most of my clients arrive without much fanfare, some make a grand entrance. Ron the Redwing, named after my father-in-law, insists upon landing on the platform first, flaring out his bright red epaulets, and bursting forth with his *o-gurglee* call. His preferred menu item is black oil sunflower seed, but the streaked brown female often uses her narrow, pointed bill to poke into the small holes of the nyjer feeder.

Are all birds welcome at Dave's Bird Bistro? Well, I have to admit that the Mourning Doves have the worst table manners by far. Not only do they actively elbow other customers, as well as one another, away from the feeders but they also leave quite a mess on the platform feeder. My wife finds them downright rude. Leaving cracked corn and white millet off the menu helps to minimize their presence, along with that of the Rock Pigeons and House Sparrows. A little pile of thick brush keeps them from feeding on the ground below the restaurant.

I certainly do not tolerate the "nasty boys." Kicking seed wastefully onto the ground and aggressively taking over the whole restaurant, grackles of any kind are just plain obnoxious around feeders. Replacing sunflower seed with white safflower seed is just about the best way to send grackles elsewhere while keeping the desired customers coming back for more.

It'll come as no surprise to some who know me that hawks and falcons are welcome at Dave's Bird Bistro anytime. After all, they've got to eat, too. And the drama is just so darn interesting.

Unlike the bistros of some other folks, however, mine is not open to nonfeathered clients, especially squirrels. I am not in the business of fattening up these critters so that they can multiply their numbers even more and raid the nests of my main clientele. That's why I employ high-quality pole baffles; avoid suet laden with seeds and fruits; offer sunflower seed in a Squirrel Buster Classic, one of the best anti-squirrel feeders in the business; and fill the platform feeder with safflower seeds, which squirrels do not like.

Finally, a quick word of advice to other maître d's out there. Operate a clean restaurant and lay on the freshest foodstuffs. Ask yourself — would you go back to an eatery that did not?

DAVID M. BIRD is professor of wildlife biology and director of the Avian Science and Conservation Centre of McGill University. A regular columnist for *Bird Watcher's*

Digest and *The Gazette* of Montreal, he is also the author or editor of several books, including *The Bird Almanac: The Ultimate Guide to Essential Facts of the World's Birds* and *Bird's Eye View*. Bird has received several awards for his conservation efforts and is a fellow of the American Ornithologists' Union.

4. *Clean Your Optics: The Unbearable Brightness of Seeing*
by Bill Thompson III

SOME YEARS AGO, an acquaintance who had just retired from a long career doing maintenance on high-end movie cameras gave me an optics cleaning kit. I thought this was nice, but I doubted I'd use it much. After all, I always had my shirttail and a bit of saliva handy to clean my old standby binoculars. Then I did a major optics upgrade and began to feel a bit more protective about my new optics and their pristine lens surfaces. I used the cleaning kit and was knocked out by the results. Really clean lenses. I immediately cleaned every pair of binoculars and glasses in my house.

A good optics cleaning kit should consist of

- a soft hair-bristle brush for whisking away dust, bread crumbs, sand, Chee-to bits, and any other abrasive particles that might damage lens coatings or surfaces when you are wiping the lenses with a cloth
- a soft cleaning cloth, preferably one designed specifically for cleaning coated glass surfaces. Lens tissues will

work, but they do not seem to get things as clean as a soft, absorbent cloth

- a small bottle of lens cleaning fluid. The fluid should also be designed for use on coated lens surfaces — no Windex please.

Most optics manufacturers sell cleaning kits with their birding optics. These kits are also available from your eye doctor, though the brush may not be included. You can find a soft hair-bristle brush at a drugstore (look for makeup brushes) or at an art-supply store (buy an inexpensive artist's brush and cut the handle short for better portability).

I always carry a cleaning kit with me in the field. One never knows where that stray dollop of mayonnaise will fall, and the old lick-the-lens-and-wipe-it-off-with-your-shirt strategy is a great way to degrade the quality of your optics. Each minute scratch diminishes the light transmission efficiency of your binocs, and over time these scratches will drive you insane.

When I lead a field trip at a birding festival, I often line everyone up for Optics Inspection. I ask the worst offenders (those with the filthiest optics) to step forward. Surprisingly, these same people are usually the most avid birders in our group. After I clean their binoculars, I enjoy hearing the shouts of wonder, joy, and astonishment, including some expletives normally reserved for sightings of Horned Guans and Ivory-billed Woodpeckers.

I'm not sure why, but I get a great buzz out of cleaning other people's optics. It's easy to do, takes just a few minutes, and the results are immediately appreciated. At a festival in West Virginia last year, a returning attendee came up to me, handed me his binoculars, and said, "Bill, I'm so happy you've got your cleaning kit again this year. As you can see, I've been saving up!" Except for the plastic toy, there was an entire Happy Meal of food on the lenses of his binoculars. "This might require a backhoe and a pressure washer," I explained. "Or you could invest in some new binoculars and a lobster bib."

My cleaning kit lives in a side pocket of my birding trip backpack. I have a smaller kit in my field guide pouch, and a lens cleaning cloth that tucks into its own little neoprene pouch clipped onto my binocular strap, so I am never without some means for cleaner lenses. Carry your cleaning kit with you on all your birding adventures, and you'll always be prepared for the unbearable brightness of seeing.

ˇ ˇ ˇ

TIPS FOR CLEANING YOUR OPTICS

- Hold the binocs up and, brushing up from underneath, use the soft hair-bristle brush to whisk off any particulate matter. Brushing from below allows you to use our friend gravity to your advantage.
- Inspect the brushed-off lenses and repeat the brushing until all crumbs and dust are removed.
- Spray a light coating of lens cleaner on your cleaning cloth and apply to the lens with a light circular motion.
- In cases of extreme lens grunge, spray the cleaner directly onto the lens and let it soak for a few seconds to loosen up anything adhered to the glass surface. Make sure your cleaning solution is intended for use with coated optics. You may need to repeat the fluid-cloth step to remove all the streaking.
- As a last step, a quick fogging breath onto the lens and a few soft swipes with the cleaning cloth will remove any streaking or residue from the cleaning solution.
- To check out your work, tilt the binocs so the light reflects off the surface (you will be looking at the lens from a 45-degree angle). Any remaining streaks will be easy to spot and attack.
- Go find some birds and enjoy your clearer, brighter, greatly improved outlook.

BILL THOMPSON III is a lifelong bird watcher, the editor of *Bird Watcher's Digest*, and the author of numerous books on birds and birding, including *Identify Yourself: The 50 Most Common Birding Identification Challenges*. He and his wife, Julie Zickefoose, live on an eighty-acre farm in southeastern Ohio with their two children, Liam and Phoebe.

5. *Bigger Is Not Better*
by Clay Sutton

AFTER AN EARLY START, we arrived at our first stop just as the clouds pulled away to reveal a crystal winter morning. Brisk northerly winds stirred the bare trees, promising that hunting raptors would soon be riding the steady breeze. Skeins of Snow Geese crisscrossed the sky, leaving south Jersey's Delaware Bay marshes for the rich bounty of inland farm fields.

I reached down for my binoculars, to the place they always lie — next to the driver's seat of my venerable minivan — and felt . . . nothing. I felt around, moving farther afield. Nothing. Slipped under the seat? Hiding under my jacket? No. Slowly came the realization that they just weren't there. Where? The panic rapidly built until I realized that no, I *hadn't* taken them into the convenience store on the mandatory predawn coffee stop. And, yes, I distinctly remembered my trusty Leicas sitting on the table by the front door, forgotten. I had gone birding without my binoculars.

As reality set in, I began to think. Heading back home wasn't an option. We were over an hour away, and this wasn't just for fun—we were on a scheduled winter raptor and waterfowl survey, gathering key data. I did have my spotting scope — good for ducks but not really the ticket for scanning for hawks and eagles; I could just use that all day. Then it hit me. Maybe I still had an old pair of binoculars buried in my van. One had been given away, another pair bartered, and one donated pair now watches hawks in Veracruz. I rummaged under the seats and behind the back seat, going through the detritus of many years afield. No, not discarded sandwich wrappers and coffee cups, or even owl pellets or mysterious feathers, but the trappings of a field naturalist — hip boots, chest waders, dip net, snake stick, sunscreen and bug spray, gloves and hats, forms and files. There were about a dozen field guides — wildflowers and trees and animals from *A* to *Z*. I might need to identify an alcid, but why was *African Mammals* in there? (Although I did once see a zebra standing among horses in a Texas pasture.)

Finally, at the bottom of all these memories, I found them — my once-prized 16 × 50 blunderbuss binoculars, which I just *had* to have soon after I began hawk watching, back around 1974. I hadn't seen them in years, but all of a sudden, up from the depths, there were the bins I had depended on for about five formative years. I felt a thrill as I realized that these fond old friends were about to save the day.

As the first Bald Eagle came sailing overhead, I lifted the heavy binoculars. Oops, fuzzy view — need to adjust the diopter. Still dark and blurry. I reached for the lens cleaning kit. Okay, now I was ready. As I put the bins on a soaring Red-tailed Hawk in the clear blue sky, it was indistinct, as if I were viewing it on a cloudy day. Were the lens coatings still okay? Check — they looked good to me. I blinked a few times and tried again. Slowly, over the course of the next few minutes, it dawned on me that the only thing wrong was that my once-coveted binoculars were, in fact, appalling — a wretched excuse for field glasses compared with today's stellar crop.

At least to some degree, we all pretty much began our birding careers with bad binoculars, but in this case I had gone from my cutting-edge Leica 8 × 42s back to my binoculars of yore without having once lifted the old pair in all the intervening years. It is a classic scenario: you don't realize how good today's Honda Civic is until you drive a boat-of-a-car 1965 Chevy Impala. Sometimes we forget how good we've got it today; such a reality check leads to an appreciation of how mightily the pioneers of birding must have struggled with the poor quality of their optics.

My own beginnings in birding are rooted in hawk watching. Since hawks are often at a great distance or height, early on I thought I needed more power — the mantra of guys for everything from autos to boats, lawn mowers to power tools. I thought that if my binoculars were just bigger and more powerful, I could see farther and identify hawks better. My first Tasco 7 × 50s soon gave way to 10 × 50s. These soon paled as I envied a friend's 12-power optics. Finally, I looked through a fellow hawk watcher's 16 × 50s, and I was helpless. A couple of paychecks and a few weeks later, the mail-order package arrived on my front stoop. Now I was ready to do some serious hawk watching!

I used these cumbersome binoculars for about five years. In some ways they *were* good for me; I didn't need to go to the gym because I was pumping iron every time I lifted them. We watched hawks together from Cape May to Hawk Mountain, Braddock Bay to the Florida Keys, Duluth to the Rio Grande Valley. We had some good times together. Yet on this recent wintry morning on the Jersey salt marsh, I felt cheated, let down. I felt slightly queasy, too, not only from the horrible view through my former friends, but also from the growing revelation that my entire birding style had been predicated on what, I now realized, were pretty bad binoculars.

Yet, figuratively, these are the sorts of binoculars that made hawk watching history — at Cape May, at Golden Gate, and beyond. This is a fondly remembered time, when the information highway first met the Kittatinny flyway, and when Cape May's emerging fame as a hawk-watching mecca met with the booming birding market in the 1970s and early 1980s. They were exciting times, but in retrospect, the binoculars that enabled it all were less than exciting.

And so I completed my winter survey. Each time I raised the old binoculars at a coursing harrier or a furtive Cooper's Hawk, it was as if I were looking through a fog, or birding at nightfall. The image was dark and murky and had little clarity. I saw no field marks, no feather features or patterns — only silhouettes, shapes, movement, and characteristic behavior. By the end of the day, I realized that, back then, the reason I had come to depend so much on GISS (general impression of size and shape) was that that was all I saw. *Hawks in Flight* might just as well have been titled *Hawks at Night*.

It's interesting now to realize that my entire style of bird identification resulted in part from using oversize binoculars that effectively put me in the dark, obscuring many field marks. Despite my current state-of-the-art Leicas, GISS is still an approach I prefer, for birds from bounding sea birds to probing peeps and twitchy warblers. Obviously I use all field marks now (at least the ones I can remember), but I back up all my bird identification with a deep-rooted dependence on GISS, the sometimes subconscious and hard to put our finger on "gestalt" of a bird.

And there you have my confession. *Hawks in Flight* might never have been written had Pete Dunne and I, and maybe David Sibley, had better binoculars. Yet in the end, I wouldn't change a thing. Indeed, the intended occurred: we did learn to identify hawks, as Pete likes to say, "at the limit of conjecture." GISS will make you a better birder, as I think it did for me, yet funnily, for this hawk watcher, it had its roots in bad binoculars.

If there is a moral to this somewhat tongue-in-cheek story, it is that bigger is not better. Even today, higher power means less light, and less light means less color, clarity, and detail. If you are a beginning birder, and particularly a new hawk watcher, avoid the pitfall of wanting to get figuratively and effectively closer to the bird. Be assured that, after my day with my ancient 16 × 50s, I am completely happy with half the magnification, my 8 × 42s. With them, I can see twice as much.

Although, you know, I did want to try out those new 10 × 40s. I hear they are pretty good. That one distant eagle yesterday might have been a Golden, and I wonder, just maybe, if I had a little more power?

CLAY SUTTON is a coauthor, with Pete Dunne and David Sibley, of the 1988 classic *Hawks in Flight*. With his wife,

Pat Sutton, he has coauthored *How to Spot Hawks and Eagles, How to Spot an Owl, How to Spot Butterflies,* and *Birds and Birding at Cape May*. He lives at Cape May, New Jersey, and is a writer, naturalist, consultant, and birding tour leader.

6. *Choose Your Wardrobe Wisely:*
Good Birders Don't Wear White
by Sheri Williamson

ON OCTOBER 14, 1991, I spent several hours crouched by a trail high in Ramsey Canyon monitoring a nest. Most birds in southeastern Arizona had fledged their young weeks or months earlier, but these were no ordinary birds. These were Eared Quetzals, then known as Eared Trogons — globally rare cousins of the Elegant Trogon — and this was the first nest of the species ever recorded in the United States. At the time, I had a feeling that these magnificent birds would change my life, but I had no idea that they would change my wardrobe as well.

These particular Eared Quetzals had arrived in the Huachuca Mountains in early August, among several that crossed the Mexican border that summer. Tantalizing reports from the Chiricahua Mountains since early June already had the birding community abuzz, so when news of this latest sighting worked its way through the grapevine, birders came flooding into Ramsey Canyon in hopes of spotting these treasures from the Sierra Madre.

Over the next three weeks, hundreds of birders braved the rugged trails and thin air, but the quetzals were maddeningly shy and disappeared into the forest at the first sign of human intrusion. For every quetzal seeker who succeeded, many more went away with nothing but the memory of faint alarm calls receding into the distance. In fact, it seemed that the more people went looking, the harder the birds were to find. Discouraged birders relayed disturbing tales of shouting, running, off-trail pursuit, and loud and continuous playing of taped calls. As the success rate declined, so did interest in chasing the birds, and by the week after Labor Day, birds again outnumbered birders in Ramsey Canyon.

Quetzal encounters continued through September, but so sporadically and so deep into the wilderness that only a few intrepid birders were willing to make the effort. Even sightings of one of the birds entering an old woodpecker hole in early September didn't spark a new episode of "quetzal mania," because it was just too late for the birds to be starting a family. Or so we thought — until October 10, when a group of visitors videotaped the female entering a cavity in a dead maple easily visible from the trail. The stakes were raised two days later, when a member of the same party returned to the site and watched as the male carried a caterpillar into the hole, confirming the presence of nestlings.

The nest was just a two-mile hike from where I lived and worked at Ramsey Canyon Preserve, so on October 14, armed with a spotting scope and notebook, I took a day off to watch the nest and record every possible detail for posterity. At 12:44, an hour since the previous feeding, several *squeal-chuck* calls signaled the arrival of the male and silenced the six birders patiently awaiting his return. After two breathless minutes, he landed at the nest entrance, only to fly immediately to a nearby tree. There he sat squeal-chucking in alarm, each call muffled by the large caterpillar in his mouth and punctuated by a flash of his white outer tail feathers.

On previous feeding visits, the arriving parent had entered the nest almost immediately, despite the presence of a small crowd of observers. So what caused this delay? Over the next eight minutes, the male quetzal flew back and forth across the clearing, calling constantly, before landing once again at the nest entrance. Through the spotting scope, I saw his head turn briefly toward the trail before he flew off again, still squealing in alarm. I followed the direction of his gaze to a recently arrived birder sitting apart from the rest but in plain view of the nest. The man's white shirt and cap glowed like a beacon against the dark forest backdrop. The problem suddenly became clear.

Though movement risked distressing the bird even more, I scuttled over to the birder in white and asked him to remove and hide his shirt and cap. Taken aback at first, he quickly complied when I explained the reason behind this odd request. I crept back to my spotting scope and notebook, and watched for six more tense minutes before the male quetzal finally entered the cavity. After less than a minute inside, he slipped away for another foraging run, returning a few minutes later with another insect. This time there was little hesitation as he disappeared into the nest to feed his young.

That evening a colleague and I cut a few yards of camo cloth into primitive ponchos for loan to inappropriately dressed quetzal watchers, allowing dozens of people to observe the nest with minimal disturbance to the parent birds. Tragically, the nestlings died in an early winter storm just two weeks later, but what we learned in that short time has raised awareness of how something as simple as a white shirt can affect the birds we watch.

Though Eared Quetzals are unusually sensitive, they are not unique. Most birds are highly visual creatures, and color plays a significant role in their lives and behavior. Elegant Trogons also flash their white tail feathers to signal alarm. A Northern Cardinal's parental instinct is triggered by the gaping orange mouths of its young. Male Red-winged Blackbirds keep the peace in winter flocks by concealing their provocative red epaulets. Blue-crowned Motmots instinctively recoil from the gaudy ringed patterns of coral snakes. As sensitive as birds are to such visual cues, is it realistic to expect them to ignore white shirts, red hats, and fluorescent yellow daypacks? Yet the average birder still doesn't give as much thought to field attire as do hunters and wildlife photographers.

Trading that white birding festival T-shirt for a camo jump suit and face paint is a little extreme, but selecting clothing in neutral colors that blend with the environment can reduce the impact of birding on birds and other wildlife and improve the birding experience for all.

———————

SHERI WILLIAMSON, author of *A Field Guide to Hummingbirds of North America* in the Peterson Field Guide Series, lives in Bisbee, Arizona. Her otherwise drab wardrobe includes a few gaudy tropical prints that she wears when visiting hummingbird hot spots and a tie-dyed Led Zeppelin T-shirt for formal occasions.

7. Question Authority: Good Birders Sometimes Wear White

by Kenn Kaufman

FOR SEVERAL YEARS, a bumper sticker on my car read, QUESTION AUTHORITY. Some guy in a parking lot once asked me what question I was an authority on, but this misinterpretation didn't discourage me. The basic premise is a good one, and I made it a central point in the introduction to my *Field Guide to Advanced Birding* (Houghton Mifflin, 1990). Good birders will always question the dictates of the experts, and with good reason: even the top experts are sometimes wrong.

I used to live in Arizona, and one winter shortly after I moved to Tucson, there was great excitement about a Streak-backed Oriole visiting feeders at a residence there. The local experts had confirmed the identification, and a number of top listers had flown in from other states to check the bird off on their life lists. I went to look at the bird, and I felt that it didn't add up. Yes, its back was buffy tan with narrow black spots, but otherwise it looked just like an adult male Hooded Oriole. With some research, we determined that it was, in fact, an adult male Hooded Oriole, in typical plumage for early winter, its solid black back mostly obscured by tan feather edges. The experts had been wrong.

There are innumerable such examples of errors by experts. Of course, everyone makes mistakes with snap identifications in the field. (I once misidentified a Brown-headed Cowbird as a rare Five-striped Sparrow in front of a whole tour group. Believe me, I was hearing about that one for a while!) But even with more time for a careful decision, groups of experienced birders can be wrong. Several of the top birders in the United States, people with superb field skills, once identified a bird as a Smith's Longspur far out of range. It was days before someone figured out that the bird was actually a Sky Lark, a member of an utterly different family. The correct identification might have come sooner if more birders had questioned the initial diagnosis.

This principle doesn't apply just to matters of identification. Experts can be wrong about all manner of bird occurrences. Years ago a Jabiru, a huge tropical species of stork, showed up in Oklahoma. Experienced birders scoffed about the record at the time, saying that this bird had to be an escapee from a zoo. But the pattern of records of Jabirus out of range in the time since then would suggest that the bird was actually a natural wild stray, moving north from nesting areas in southeastern Mexico. Similarly, many years ago there were a couple of records of birds that were probably Green Violet-ears, big tropical hummingbirds, in a state that shall be nameless. The authorities yawned, pointing out that violet-ears never had been found north of Mexico except for a limited area in southern Texas. Since then, stray Green Violet-ears have been documented in more than a dozen states and even in two Canadian provinces, suggesting that these first sightings would have been totally plausible.

Even matters of birding technique can be subject to major differences of opinion. To name one prominent example, what about the idea that good birders don't wear white in the field? Is that sound advice? Well, sometimes. My friends Sheri Williamson and Tom Wood were able to document the fact that one pair of rare Eared Quetzals in Arizona reacted with extreme alarm to anyone wearing white. Certainly, in that one canyon, birders were well advised not to wear white. And if you are going out alone to stalk shy birds in the forest undergrowth, you'd best wear dark, muted colors. But there are many kinds of birding situations — such as hawk watching on high ridges, shore birding on wide-open flats, gull watching at garbage dumps, seeking of pelagic birds on boat trips at sea, et cetera — in which the color of your apparel makes no difference. In many parks and refuges, birds become so accustomed to humans that they stop paying us any attention at all, except as occasional sources of food. In such a situation, you can wear full-body camo and it won't get you an inch closer to the birds than if you were wearing a neon orange jump suit. The birds can see you regardless of what you're wearing, and they just don't care.

Many of us have a tendency to believe what we read, as if things put in print would be more reliable, but that isn't always so. The Internet as a source is particularly suspect. I recently did an informal survey which indicated that nearly half the bird-related information available on-line is incorrect or incomplete. But even information printed in magazines or books, even if they're written by expert birders, may turn out to be wrong. My example involving a Hooded Oriole misidentified as a Streak-backed Oriole years ago was not entirely the fault of the birders who made the error: they were consulting books that helped lead them astray. Even today, more than a quarter century later, there are books which will tell you that a Hooded Oriole always has a solidly colored back, so a similar bird with a "beaded" pattern on the back would be a Streak-backed. Even with the advances in knowledge in recent years, birders still need to question what they're told.

Am I saying, then, that good birders will always question authority? No, not quite. If a section of a wildlife refuge is closed to entry, or if an area is off-limits to the use of tape recordings, or if a tract of land is posted "No trespassing," good birders will always heed that kind of authority. Our independent, break-the-rules approach will always be trumped by the demands of birding ethics. Aside from that, though, anything is fair game. Question what you read and what you're told. Even if your investigation only proves that the experts were right about some fact, you'll have the pleasure of knowing that fact, really knowing it, from your own experience.

KENN KAUFMAN is the originator of the Kaufman Field Guide series. A devoted conservationist, he works vigorously to promote the appreciation and protection of nature. He is a field editor for *Audubon* and a columnist for numerous magazines. Kaufman is the author of *Lives of North American Birds*, the *Peterson Field Guide to Advanced Birding*, and *Kingbird Highway*.

8. *Avoid False Starts*

by Jeffrey A. Gordon

THERE IS NO SANTA CLAUS. As much as we would like to believe there is, there isn't. It's a fact we all must face at some point, lest we doom ourselves to perpetual disappointment.

Now brace yourself. I aim to bring down one of birding's great shibboleths, a commonly held belief so simple and seductive that many longtime birders who should know better cannot bring themselves to admit its essential inaccuracy. But I swear to you, dumping this romantic notion right now will make you a much happier birder in the long run.

So get ready for a stiff shot of truth. I'm going to give it to you straight, no chaser. Here it is: *The name of a bird will not tell you what it looks like.*

I know, I know, it hurts a little. Breathe. Give yourself a moment to adjust. It's a lot to take in.

"But wait," you may say. "Isn't a Red-winged Blackbird a black bird with red wings?" Well, yes, I'll admit that it is, though the curmudgeon in me feels compelled to point out that those wings are in fact mostly black, with red only on the shoulders, and that those red shoulders usually have yellow borders that pass completely without comment. But okay, I concede. It's a good, visually descriptive name.

The difficult truth remains. For every time the nomenclature keeps its promises, it'll break your heart a hundred times over. For every winner, such as Roseate Spoonbill, applied to a bright pink bird with a distinctive, spoon-shaped bill, there are dozens of clunkers, such as Ring-necked Duck, Red-bellied Woodpecker, Purple Sandpiper, and Orange-crowned Warbler — species you could observe fifty times each and never once see the features for which they are named.

Other names, while technically accurate, are too general to be really helpful. Of the seven species of chickadee, five have black caps, but only one is properly called Black-capped Chickadee. Yellow-bellied Flycatcher? Don't ask.

I'd like to say that bird names are misleading with respect to appearance only, but it doesn't stop there. Time for a quick quiz: where would you go to have the best chance at finding a Connecticut Warbler, a Philadelphia Vireo, or a Nashville Warbler? The answers: not Connecticut, not Philadelphia, and not Nashville, respectively.

There is one more big way bird names will confound you, and it is perhaps the most insidious. Here goes. In North America, we have a tame orange-breasted bird commonly seen around houses and in yards. We call it a robin, an American Robin. In England, they also have a familiar orange-breasted yard bird that they also call a robin. Just "Robin," or "the Robin." You might think these two robins would be somehow related in a taxonomic sense, but they are not. They're no closer to each other than a mockingbird is to a wren.

The Brits do have a close cousin of the American Robin, however. It is called the Blackbird. The Blackbird is known for its habit of nocturnal singing, which the Beatles immortalized in song.

Now everybody knows that, in North America, we have a lot of blackbirds. Red-winged Blackbirds, Yellow-headed Blackbirds, Rusty Blackbirds, and Brewer's Blackbirds. But none of them is biologically close to Britain's Blackbird.

Our North American blackbirds do have some close cousins that may surprise you, though. That incandescent oriole weaving its nest in the treetops just outside? It's nothing more (and nothing less) than a blackbird with a lot of orange on it. Those meadowlarks whose song wafts sweetly in over the fields? All blackbirds. But the starlings in the park — noisy, aggressive, gregarious, and mostly black — they aren't blackbirds at all. They're related to myna birds, the famous pet store mimics that ornithologists know as the Hill Myna.

If you're still reading, rather than looking for another hobby entirely, you're probably wondering how this mess happened. Why are bird names so bad? Why don't they make it easier to learn birds, not harder?

I do have some answers for you, and I hope they will set your mind at least partially at ease. A lot of the naming of birds was done by museum scientists looking at museum specimens, not by observers in the field. And things that seem quite distinctive when a bird is in your hands are often invisible when it is in the bush.

So Red-bellied Woodpeckers do have red bellies, after all. But they are usually obscured by the tree trunk on which the woodpecker perches. Ring-necked Ducks actually have iridescent maroon neck rings, but they're subtle. The museum origin of names also explains arcane oddities, such as Semipalmated Sandpiper and Semipalmated Plover — in the hand, their partially webbed, or semipalmate, toes are excellent means of identifying them.

What of the Connecticut Warbler? Why can't I hop a plane to Hartford and see one any day of the year? Often, the names of birds memorialize the spots where the first specimens were collected, and those may or may not be places where the species are numerous or frequently seen. But the first of these warblers to make its way into an ornithologist's hands was collected in the Constitution State, so there you have it.

And as for the mysteries of orange blackbirds, unrelated robins, and so on, such tangles are typically results of the basic human desire to relate new things to familiar things from back home, even if doing so is a bit of a stretch. If you get to the point when you want to know precise biological affinities, turn to the scientific names, which make relationships clear.

Finally, as much as I've advised you to be wary of common names, I also suggest you embrace them in all their wackiness and idiosyncrasy. There have been numerous attempts to "rationalize" them, and they have all been failures, accomplishing little except draining the considerable poetry and charm our names for birds do have. Just don't ask more of them than they can provide. You might as well look for Saint Nick to come sliding down your chimney.

JEFFREY A. GORDON is a writer, tour leader, and naturalist who lives in Lewes, Delaware. He serves as field editor for *Bird Watcher's Digest* and is a frequent speaker at various birding and nature festivals. For more information on Gordon's activities, visit www.jeffreyagordon.com.

9. *Take Field Notes*

by Jessie H. Barry

OBSERVATION IS THE KEY to bird identification. The abilities to watch carefully, discern differences between individuals, notice what makes an individual unique, and draw a conclusion to link the individual to a species are essential for a good birder. One of the best ways to improve your observation skills is to take notes in the field. The process of writing and sketching what you observe will help you retain what you learn. You will find yourself discovering marks you've never noticed before. Keeping field notes can be a very rewarding experience. It not only sharpens your birding skills but also provides a record for future reference, and it contributes to the scientific community. While taking field notes can be challenging and tedious at times, it also sends you skyrocketing up the learning curve!

Field notebooks come in all shapes and styles. You may prefer pocket-size over larger formats, lined or unlined, pen versus pencil, spiral or hardbound. (Steer clear of pencil in spiral-bound notebooks, however, as it is prone to smear over time.) Whatever format you choose, what's most important is to develop a system of note taking that suits your interests and to use it often; get in the habit of taking a notebook with you each time you head into the field.

In their most basic form, field notes include a list of species seen from a particular location on a certain date. It is important to go a step further by adding the number of individuals of each species as well as a breakdown of sex and age ratios. These quantifications make lists tremendously more valuable, because they provide considerably more information. For example, there is a big difference between one and one hundred White-rumped Sandpipers, and a number provides a reference point for the relative abundance of the species. Each notebook page should include a header with your name and the date. Incorporate the time and duration of your observations and the location. Location should have specifics, such as country or state, county, city, street, elevation, or place name. For example, a locality may read, "New Jersey, Cape May County, Cape May Point, hawk-watch platform." Weather conditions are also essential, because weather can have a great impact on what you see or don't see. Is it warm, sunny with light wind from the southwest, or cold with a biting northwest wind? Habitat descriptions are also valuable. They can be very simple, such as "coniferous forest" or "desert scrub," but the more specifics the better. How about adding "mature Douglas fir forest, 20% ponderosa pine with few oaks" or "mesquite flats with creosote and scattered yucca"? Additionally, if you are birding with other people, jot down their names.

Notes on what birds are doing and what they look like constitute the heart of a field notebook. Behavior descriptions often include what birds are eating, the strategies they use to obtain their food, and how they interact with one another. It's also important to include details of plumage, molt, structure, size, flight style, and soft part coloration. You never know what sorts of details you may find interesting five or ten years from now.

Sketching can be intimidating, but even crude sketches may be valuable. Draw what you see, not what you know. You may realize how little you actually were able to observe on the bird, but this process prevents you from recording field marks that you only think should be there and forces you to really study individuals. It will kick your birding skills up a couple of notches! Follow these basic guidelines for sketching. When you start drawing a bird, break it down into simple shapes. Heads are generally round, and bodies are typically oval. So, start with a circular head and an oval body, and add lines for a tail and a bill. This is the time to check your proportions, before you add details. See that you have the right size head in relation to the body, the appropriate tail length, bill size, and wing length. When adding an eye, note that the bottom of the eye lines up with the gape (where the upper and lower mandibles meet), except on waterfowl. To keep your bird from looking as if it's going to fall over, draw an imaginary line from the back of the head straight down, so that you can align the toes with the back of the head. Next, modify these shapes to form an outline of the bird and add the details as you see them. You may look back on some of your first attempts and wonder if a four-year-old could have done better. While it can be frustrating, don't get discouraged! You will be surprised at how quickly you improve if you practice regularly. If you find your sketches are not improving, try using detailed verbal description to paint word pictures instead.

Field notes, whether sketches or descriptions, can play a role in the documentation of rare birds. If you find a bird outside its normal range, good field notes and sketches (along with photographs, ideally) can be submitted to your state's bird records committee and will contribute to our knowledge of bird status and distribution.

You can also add to our collective wisdom by logging your sightings into an on-line database, such as Cornell Lab of Ornithology's eBird (www.eBird.org), which contributes to a large-scale project that tracks status, distribution, and movements across the continent. Just remember that, while computers ease the rigors of keeping lists, allowing you to enter your sightings into spreadsheets at home and PDAs in the field, they are no substitutions for sketches and written descriptions. Good birders take field notes!

———————

JESSIE H. BARRY is an undergraduate at the University of Washington, majoring in ecology and evolutionary biology. Her work has appeared in various publications, including National Geographic's *Complete Birds of North America* and *Birding* and *WildBird* magazines. Barry is a member of the Washington Bird Records Committee.

10. *Follow These Rules to See a Mangrove Cuckoo*
by Don and Lillian Stokes

ALTHOUGH THE NAME Mangrove Cuckoo may sound a little funny, this is a very serious bird. Make no mistake.

Because it is pretty much restricted to living and breeding in the dense and impenetrable mangroves of southern Florida, it is a hard bird to find, especially during the nonbreeding season, when it is quiet. We have had the good fortune to spend the last ten winters on Sanibel Island, Florida, where the famous Ding Darling National Wildlife Refuge is located. This is a good spot to find Mangrove Cuckoos, and we have had many opportunities to see them.

This, however, does not mean that they are easy to see. We know many people who have been coming to Ding Darling for the past twenty years and still have not seen their first Mangrove Cuckoo.

Because we have had a number of sightings, we have slowly built up a series of guidelines for those who would like to add a Mangrove Cuckoo to their life list. You might call them our six rules for increasing your chances of seeing a Mangrove Cuckoo. You will no doubt notice

the cautionary phrase "increasing your chances." There are no guarantees.

RULE 1:
Never go looking for it.

This is not a hard-and-fast rule, but in general, *trying* to find a Mangrove Cuckoo never works. One exception is notable. On a birding trip with friends, Lillian and another woman decided to get out of the car and walk through a portion of Ding Darling specifically to look for the Mangrove Cuckoo. The woman's husband and some other birders went driving ahead on the one-way refuge road; their parting words were "You'll never find a Mangrove Cuckoo."

No sooner was the car out of sight than a Mangrove Cuckoo flew across the road directly in front of the two women and landed right over their heads. They had a fabulous point-blank view for about ten minutes. Lillian's friend tried to reach her husband through a walkie-talkie but could not get through. (It turned out they were on different channels.)

A passerby agreed to find the husband and tell him the news. Later he told us how he greeted the husband: "I have good news and bad news. The good news is your wife is fine; the bad news is she found a Mangrove Cuckoo and you were not there."

RULE 2:
Never say the bird's name.

Mangrove Cuckoos have an uncanny ability to sense when someone is trying to conjure them up and thus disappear. "The bird who shall not be named" is our recommended substitute for the name Mangrove Cuckoo. Practice saying it in the house before you go out.

RULE 3:
Never go out with someone who has been looking for the Mangrove Cuckoo for twenty years with no success.

This is simple logic. If this person has not seen the bird in twenty years, he is a jinx. There is no way around it. Tell him to go look for the cuckoo on his own, preferably on a day other than when you are birding.

RULE 4:
Your chances of finding a Mangrove Cuckoo are increased if you have a nonbirder with you, preferably someone who has never even heard of a Mangrove Cuckoo.

Invariably, Mangrove Cuckoo sightings are made by non-birders, thus proving the life-is-not-fair rule. She has come along on a trip to the refuge to have you share your wisdom about birds. She does not have binoculars (even if she does, you may want to take them away). You are usually standing somewhere expounding about some heron or warbler in the mangroves when she points behind your head and says, "What's that bird?"

When you see it, you become speechless and start gesturing wildly, and your jaw drops. Finally you start sputtering things like, "This is really rare. I can't believe you found it. This is amazing. And did I mention, I can't believe you found it?" She is usually more amazed by your reaction than by the bird itself and wonders why you are babbling on about such a fairly drab and seemingly tame species.

Even when you tell her that this sighting carries unbelievable bragging rights with other birders, she seems unimpressed.

RULE 5:
Once you spot a Mangrove Cuckoo, sit back and relax.

For such elusive birds, Mangrove Cuckoos seem surprisingly unconcerned about being watched. They can often be approached to within a few yards as they walk among the tree branches, much the way parrots do, for they also have two toes in front and two behind. They eat caterpillars and so do not have to be very quick. Usually, they just move slowly from branch to branch looking under leaves.

This is part of the reason they are so hard to find. You can be looking at a densely leaved mangrove forest and a Mangrove Cuckoo can be sitting right in front of you, not moving. It most often gets your attention when it has taken a short flight across an opening and you notice its long tail, brownish gray upper parts, and buffy belly. When it lands, you can take your time observing it and calling over others to see it.

RULE 6:
If you are married to a birder, never see the Mangrove Cuckoo without your spouse.

We know many birder marriages that have temporarily faltered or, at least, been severely strained by one member catching a glimpse of this rare bird without the other present. In fact, if you have just seen a Mangrove Cuckoo without your birder-spouse, you might want seriously to consider just keeping it to yourself. When the time comes that you both see one together, still say nothing about the earlier sighting — just look as surprised as you can.

For example, the day Don first saw a Mangrove Cuckoo, Lillian was not with him for the few minutes that the bird was in view. Things were very quiet after he foolishly told her that he had just seen the Mangrove Cuckoo, expecting her to share in his joy.

Later that evening, looking at the sunset from the beach, Lillian exclaimed, "Look! The green flash!" Don mistakenly looked over to his right and missed the green flash — an incredibly rare phenomenon of a burst of green light that occurs for a second just as the sun slips below the horizon. To this day, Don has not seen a green flash, but Lillian has had many sightings of Mangrove Cuckoos. Make of this what you will, but Don is still entertaining the thought that he is working off a curse from "the bird who shall not be named."

To sum it all up, even if you do follow our rules to the letter, as a wise birder once said, "You don't find a Mangrove Cuckoo, a Mangrove Cuckoo finds you!"

———

DON AND LILLIAN STOKES are TV personalities and authors of more than thirty best-selling books, including *Stokes Field Guide to Birds*. Their PBS TV series was seen by 40 million viewers.

11. *Surrender! (Or at Least Wave a White Flag)*
by Dave Jasper

W E'VE ALL FOUND OURSELVES, typically on a nippy and breezy fall or winter day, standing on the shore of a lake or reservoir, or even out on a seawall, straining to identify distant waterfowl. Our scope isn't powerful enough or the chop and surf give just fleeting glimpses of loons, grebes, and diving ducks "corking" up and down in the distance — if only they were closer.

This is a good time to try an old technique I've been using successfully for many years. We obviously do not wear white in the woods while bird watching, but white can be used to attract loons, grebes, and diving ducks. Use a white cloth, such as a towel or scarf, and wave it back and forth, side to side over your head for a minute or so, then pause and repeat, then pause again and watch what happens with those distant dots. Goldeneyes, Buffleheads, some grebe species, and especially loons are positively curious about white and will swim toward the waving cloth.

On many occasions, I've had loons approach to within twenty yards, even vocalizing when I waved the cloth and silencing when I stopped. Barrow's and Common Goldeneyes also swim toward a white cloth waved overhead, as do Western and Clark's Grebes. I've had less success with ducks and small grebes, but any species of waterfowl anywhere may respond, so give it a try.

I've been told by British and Danish birders that they've had success bringing in owls at night by waving a smaller, hankie-size white cloth. I've had some success with Whiskered and Western Screech-Owls using this technique, and biologists and hunters know that pronghorns and Snow Geese are attracted to a waving white flag. So, wearing white clothing in the woods is a no-no, but waving white in the right situation can be most effective.

———————

DAVE JASPER has worked for the last fifteen years as a naturalist guide out of Portal, Arizona, and the adjoining Chiricahua Mountains. He has extensive experience conducting avian and botanical research projects for the Bureau of Land Management, U.S. Forest Service, National Park Service, and Colorado Division of Wildlife. His property and bird feeders in Portal are open to the public and are visited by over three thousand people yearly. Jasper delights in sharing his knowledge with all nature enthusiasts.

12. *Bird by Impression*
by Kevin Karlson

L IKE A FLASH OF LIGHTNING, several birds exploded past a group of startled birders. "What the heck was that?" was the response from most of the crowd. There was no time to study field marks, so frustration over a lost identification began to grow. A lone voice suddenly spoke up. "Snipe," she said quietly. "They were snipe."

Disbelief reigned supreme, and some shared disparaging remarks. "Now how did you come to that conclusion?" the accomplished, unappointed leader of this casual group gently asked. "Long, slender, pointed wings; medium size; whistling wing noise; and fast, zigzag flight" was her response. The leader nodded, acknowledging the accuracy of the description. These types of quick, yet accurate, field observations are becoming more common as birders use carefully applied impressions for initial field identification.

Before coauthoring *The Shorebird Guide,* I would probably have reacted as the accomplished leader did, despairing that I could not use traditional analytic field methods to identify birds in that situation. But now I'm much more like the lone voice in my anecdote, employing a simpler, impression-based approach and identifying even more birds as a result.

Birding by impression is similar in approach to the familiar "jizz" or "GISS" birding style (for general impression of size and shape). However, this approach incorporates other supporting factors, such as habitat use, behavior, overall coloration, and vocalizations, to complete a surprisingly accurate picture of each bird in an instant. Another important aspect of this approach is direct comparison with nearby birds, especially familiar ones, to determine impressions of size, shape, and structure (although these words can be synonymous, *structure* is used for descriptions of individual body parts and *shape* for overall body configuration). Direct comparison with very similar species is the best way to pinpoint subtle differences in size, structure, and plumage. It is very rewarding to find that similar species previously thought nearly impossible to identify in the field are actually separable using simple observations of shape and structure along with other impressions.

Birding by impression works best if you observe several basic, nonchangeable features. Don't rely on just one or two features to form your identification; use all available impressions to come to your conclusion. Start by forming detailed impressions of birds in your backyard, and use them as benchmarks for sizing and comparing unfamiliar birds you see later. After time, your knowledge of species information will be very thorough, with only unfamiliar birds requiring new sets of impressions. You'll find the process of identification becoming almost subconscious, and you'll instantly recognize familiar birds, while unfamiliar ones are put to the scrutiny of a fine-tuned, impression-based discipline. Conventional plumage and scientific analysis can always be applied to more complicated identification situations, with a synthesis of both disciplines resulting in a more complete picture.

There is great satisfaction in knowing you have joined an elite group capable of correctly identifying birds in difficult situations. So have fun practicing this approach everywhere you go, since that is what birding is really about!

KEVIN KARLSON has been a wildlife photographer for twenty-seven years. He is a member of the advisory board of *WildBird* magazine, a staff contributor of the column "Birder's ID," and a coauthor of *The Shorebird Guide.* Active in the Cape May birding community and member of the New Jersey Bird Records Committee for twelve years, he is the founder and president of Jaeger Tours, a small birding tour company (www.jaegertours.net) with an emphasis on the enjoyment of a total birding and nature experience.

Come Fly with Me

13. *Choose a Birding Tour Carefully*
by Victor Emanuel

AN ORGANIZED BIRDING tour can be a rewarding, educational, and fun experience if you pick a tour run by a company that is reputable and whose approach to birding is similar to your own.

Some tour companies cater to people whose exclusive goal is to see as many life birds as possible. Such trips operate at a level of intensity that some people would find exhausting, with very early departures and very long hours in the field. Other tour companies operate at a pace that enables participants to see and enjoy a long list of birds and other creatures without becoming worn down.

Ask a tour company about their approach to birding and inquire about the hours in the field. Do they normally have breakfast at 5:30 or 6:00 A.M., often have a short midday break after lunch, and return from afternoon birding by 4:00 or 5:00 P.M., or will they have breakfast at 4:30 A.M. and then stay in the field until 7:00 P.M., with dinner at 8:00, followed by owling? It is important to pick a tour whose pace is appropriate for you.

The key element in any tour is the leadership. It is useful in making a choice to know how many times a leader has operated that particular tour. A good leader needs to know intimately the areas you will visit, be familiar with the birds you might encounter, know how to find them, and most important, know how to tell others where they are. Directions such as "It is in that green tree" are not helpful. Knowing how to tell others where a bird is located is a skill acquired only after years of experience.

A good leader also needs to be skilled at handling the logistics of a tour and dealing with unexpected events (overbooked hotels, weather situations, vehicle breakdowns, and illness of a participant). Some individuals have these skills as part of their nature, but most leaders acquire such skills by gaining experience over the years.

Finally, a good leader needs to possess people skills, including the ability to communicate with and relate to a wide variety of people. It is the leader's job to do everything possible to ensure that every participant has the most enjoyable and rewarding birding experience. One of the most important attributes of a leader is enthusiasm for birds and nature. A good leader communicates to every participant information on field marks and identification, as well as life history information. Some leaders are interested only in birds, while others are interested in all aspects of natural history.

It's also a good idea to pick a tour with an itinerary that fits your approach to travel. Some people like to cover as much ground as possible, visiting, for example, five locations during a nine-day trip. This approach requires a number of one-night stays with a lot of time in transit. Other people enjoy staying at only one or two locations on a nine-day trip, so they can have several days and nights at each place.

When choosing a trip, some people focus on the cost per day and pick the least expensive. Whereas this approach may work for buying an airline ticket, it is a bad idea for choosing a birding tour. A cheaper tour probably stays in cheaper accommodations, packs more participants into a vehicle, uses a cheaper local operator, and has less experienced guides.

An organized tour is not something every birder wants to do, but for many a well-chosen tour is a hassle-free and very rewarding way to bird another part of our country or a foreign country with expert leaders and an enjoyable group of fellow birders.

———————————

VICTOR EMANUEL started birding in Texas fifty-eight years ago, at the age of eight. His travels have taken him to all the continents. He derives great pleasure from seeing and hearing birds and sharing with others these avian sights and sounds.

14. *Hug Your Tour Leader*

by Judith A. Toups

BACK WHEN OUR household added up to eight humans plus two shaggy dogs and an assortment of cats, the bloodlines of which could be traced to beloveds named Petite Chou and Rory (and thus considered venerable family retainers), a year of skimming from the grocery money wouldn't have taken me to Carencro, Louisiana, let alone to south Texas or southeast Arizona — divine destinations of which I, as a birder, would never get enough.

Humility aside, and with assists from the latest bird-finding guides, I was on fairly personal terms with the hot spots of Texas and Arizona, but travel-in-style money was almost always beyond reach. To be even more candid, I had had it up to here with tent camping, basin baths, honey pots, canvas-crashing peccaries and spotted skunks, and those dreadful desert delights and mountain medleys (euphemisms for various fire-pit stews and other burnt offerings).

Thought I, There has to be another way.

So why not become a tour leader? After all, my portfolio, if I had kept such a thing, would have highlighted years of leading students and Elderhostel groups into the hinterlands of south Mississippi in search of birds. If pressed, I could have mentioned that there was also a one-day stint as next in line to head tour guide of a high-profile birding tour company, during which I subbed for a missing leader (and in the course of which I resolved never to carry luggage for even one able-bodied, high-toned gent who took me for a gofer and not a tour guide). Besides, I knew how to drive a fifteen-passenger van.

The premise was simple, and the plan was brilliant, sort of. At a ridiculously low price per person, I would invite the participation of those whom I loved, liked, or merely tolerated if they would agree to play nice and hoist their own luggage. I would get my expense-paid trips in exchange for whatever talents I could bring to bird finding, travel logistics, food prep, and long-distance driving.

The first trip was an all-girl thing. It went swimmingly until we discovered that nine otherwise independent females could not raise a fifteen-passenger van out of a muddy ditch without help from a couple of swarthy characters in a winch-equipped pickup truck.

That trip led to a second, which was coed. The stage for disaster was set before we left town. Logistics went out the window (actually, they went out the door) when, after the ninth passenger was loaded, the side door flew right off the van (small revenge in watching the rental manager transfer all that stuff, single-handedly, into another van).

Perhaps I should mention here that we had hardly cleared Baton Rouge when a six-lane chemical spill caused a detour through several one-horse towns with multiple traffic lights.

What happened next was even worse. After a short night's sleep, each of us (I went first) had tossed luggage, food, and beverage to last a week, and our birding gear, into the van. Only then did we discover that the ignition key was exactly where I had put it — under the mountain of stuff we had just finished loading. It was high noon before I had earned the first sort of grudging forgiveness.

On day two of this escalating miscue, we lingered too long over birds of the Bolivar Peninsula, so it followed we should arrive at our next stop, a choice restaurant, a scant half-hour before closing. To save face, and time, I dropped everyone off there and went in search of the motel, so that my charges would be preregistered and they could get straight to bed. It was the least I could do.

Toups's Cheep Tours unInc. was nothing if not consistent; as I wandered the darkened streets in search of neon lights and vacancy signs, how could I have known I was looking for a motel that had burned to the ground a month earlier? It was 11:00 P.M. before everyone was settled into new digs, and as just punishment, I went to bed hungry. I have only this to say: there were mitigating circumstances.

Throughout the ensuing years, it was the unforeseen,

and the unimaginable, that dogged me every time we headed west. How could I know beforehand that the motel chain I had chosen for three nightly stops en route to Arizona would be greeting guests with signs proclaiming that we should pardon their mess while they made renovations for our future comfort? Who could have guessed that Los Tres Vaqueros, the only Tex-Mex café within fifteen miles of our motel, would be closed on a Thursday. On a Thursday!

Who would have thought that the sunny firmament and dry, dusty ground that eased our way out to the one parking slot near California Gulch (with its exalted Five-striped Sparrow) would turn violent on us? Just before the gulch bottomed out, the sparrow was ours. But then the sky clouded over and delivered a deluge that obliterated all traces of the primitive road we had followed earlier. We were, in a word, clueless, and a couple of hours later than checkout time at our Nogales motel.

Once we were under way again, Murphy's Law went into a full gallop. The great birding area at Kino Springs, so fondly remembered, had been plowed under and then built over (scratch those Tropical Kingbirds). Then the van developed a persistent cough and was coaxed and prodded to the only garage in Patagonia; repairs would take twenty-four hours and seven hundred dollars for parts and labor.

Patagonia is an intriguing place, if one has wheels. But

shank's mare will not take one far enough to save the day. Not more than five miles west, there's a legendary rest stop, and just across the road from there lives, or lived, the Rose-throated Becard, a most-wanted bird that would have brought me some measure of redemption, if not a few re-sounding accolades.

Fortunately, local color, fine dining, and alcoholic bev-erages were within walking distance, at a very pricey joint known as The Purple Elvis. We engaged in gluttony and sloshed away our sorrows, and for another three hundred dollars and change I bought my way out of the worst batch of witches' brew that the fates could have cooked up.

That was the last bubbling cauldron I could handle. It's fair to say that I never made a dime that didn't wind up in the pot of retribution. After fifteen years of winter trips to Texas and summer trips to Arizona, I had (most gratefully) aged out of the birding tour business. There is nothing left to say. Except this: Don't forget to hug your tour guide.

———

Judith A. Toups, coauthor of two birding guides, has written a weekly column for thirty-two years. Her work also appears in many birding magazines. She revels in teaching birding skills to novices, known as the Bush-whackers, who celebrate good days in the field with noto-riously bad performances of the Life-bird Macarena.

15. *Think Like a Migrating Bird*
by Amy K. Hooper

BEFORE WE TRAVEL to bird, we need to think like a bird that's going to fly hundreds, if not thousands, of miles. Bristle-thighed Curlews, for example, fly non-stop for more than four thousand miles while migrating. Thank goodness we don't have to rely on our own man-power every time we want to travel for birding! Even when we attend festivals with field trips that make birding logistically easier, we should take responsibility for a few aspects.

To prepare ourselves physically, we need to consider our ability to bird for hours in the middle of nowhere or with limited facilities. Many birds eat like the dickens before migration, and Blackpoll Warblers even double their weight before taking to the air. We needn't go to that extreme, but we'd be better off if we made somewhat similar efforts.

The week before leaving home turf, make an effort to drink more water than usual. Most nutritional information recommends at least eight 8-ounce glasses of pure water every day. If you venture outdoors with a hydrated body, you're less likely to run out of energy too soon. And I do mean water — not coffee, soda, or beer! No matter how tasty, those beverages don't help our bodies prepare for outdoor excursions because of their diuretic properties.

During your preparatory week, spend a few more hours in bed — not reading, talking, or watching television, but sleeping. If you add thirty to sixty minutes of shuteye each night, you'll feel better rested going into your adventure. To fuel your body during the upcoming excursion, pack very portable snacks — such as unsalted nuts, fresh and dried fruits and vegetables, and low-fat granola bars — to supplement your meals. If you eat small servings of protein, simple sugars, and carbohydrates throughout the day, your body will receive the nutrients that it needs to keep moving. For each day, consider taking a quarter cup of almonds, an apple, six dried apricots, twelve baby carrot sticks, and a granola bar. With the extra physical effort that active birding can demand, you'll benefit from the healthy fuel-ups.

Also remember to take bottled water each time you head out the door, even when attending a festival. While some events provide bottled water for field-trip participants, some do not. You're better off assuming that the leaders have not stashed a cooler of agua in the bus's storage compartment or in the boat's cabin.

In fact, always act inquisitively and poke around like a bird while traveling. During one festival, I sat in front of a couple who had assumed that the field-trip leader had transferred all the food onto the bus. Rather than investigate the lit-up room from which the participants had collected their previously ordered lunches, the couple had walked straight from their car to the bus. While the rest of us later munched on sandwiches, chips, cookies, and fruit, they nibbled on very limited provisions. Perhaps if they'd thought like migrating blackpolls, their stomachs wouldn't have grumbled so much!

———————————————

Amy K. Hooper edits *WildBird* in Southern California and travels regularly to birding events around the country. She learned the value of these travel tips the hard way and never leaves home without a snack stash.

16. Don't Be Afraid of Two-thirds of the Planet: Pelagic Birding
by Steve Howell

P ELAGICS ARE BIRDING TRIPS in boats that head offshore, usually for the day. They're increasingly popular because they allow birders to see species that usually occur out of sight of mainland — albatross, petrels, storm-petrels, as well as whales, dolphins, flying fish, sea turtles, and . . . It's another world out there, a magical world where anything is possible. Imagine . . . *Black-footed Albatross sailing effortlessly over sunny blue waters and landing to swim within a few feet of the boat, whinnying and bickering over scraps . . . Black-capped Petrels wheeling in rollercoaster arcs and with them, what the . . . a smaller petrel — a Bermuda Petrel, a birding grail, and you're watching it . . . blizzards of Sabine's Gulls and Arctic Terns scattered by falconlike Long-tailed Jaegers, and all feeding over countless Cassin's Auklets popping up like corks amid lunge-feeding blue whales, and then the waters cut by a passing school of northern right whale dolphins, and then . . . a big storm-petrel — a Band-rumped — bounding through a mass of fluttering little Wilson's Storm-Petrels, like so many butterflies pattering on the slick sea surface . . .*

So much to see, so unpredictable, and so little time — pelagics can be addictive, so wonderful, so why would anyone be afraid of them? I really hate seasickness — not the reality but the hype. I think most people do not, in fact, get seasick, but the attendant fear-generating media would do any political administration proud. I've been seasick once in twenty-five years of pelagic birding — hey, I'll try anything once. I didn't like it, and I have worked, successfully, on avoiding it ever since. So you probably can, too.

That said, some people really do get seasick easily — and conversely, maybe some people are immune to seasickness. If you think you're immune, try this: wait till you have a bad cold or flu, then party all night and drink a lot of alcohol, get maybe an hour of sleep, and then board a boat for a pelagic. But you're not through yet. Wait until the boat is rolling around and go sit in the head — preferably with diesel fumes leaking in — put on sunglasses, look down, and try reading a foreign-language text. If you can get past a page of reading without feeling nauseated, then congratulations.

So that's how to get seasick; now think of the opposite. Try to avoid illnesses and other things that weaken your system, get a good night's sleep, don't drink too much the night before, stay out of the cabin or confined spaces where fresh air doesn't circulate, maintain clear vision, and don't attempt to read anything (spend some time beforehand reviewing the birds you might see). Try to stay warm (but not too warm); take rain gear even if it's a nice day — the ocean is cooler than the land and weather changes; wear sunglasses to reduce eyestrain; apply sunscreen even if it's cloudy; use pockets for drinks and food (so you are independent of the cabin); have a zipper-lock bag handy with dry tissues to keep your binoculars clean; and take earplugs — the engine noise can be distracting on some boats, if not actually damaging to your hearing. Okay, so those are the basics, but what else is there, what gives experienced sea birders the edge? Here are five extra tips for your first pelagic.

1. DON'T USE DRUGS

If you don't know whether you get seasick, then don't assume you do — chances are you won't, especially if you try not to. Some drugs for seasickness make you sleepy and dry-mouthed and give you headaches — things you really don't need. You're better off trying your first trip free from drugs that might disqualify an athlete from competing, and that can inhibit your enjoyment of the trip.

2. DON'T HOLD ON

What? Contrary to what you may think, ocean motion has a finite number of basic modes; learning to move in rhythm with these is the single biggest help to enjoying the ocean. Watch the wave direction and balance yourself without holding on — but always keep within reach of a rail, and start out with gentle seas. If you can stand free on deck, you will have two hands to hold your binoculars. After a while you'll stand without even thinking of the wave motion; you might as well be on land.

3. DON'T USE BINOCULARS

Huh? Well, sometimes, but mostly use your naked eye to observe shapes and overall patterns and watch flight styles and equate them to wind direction and wind speed. Sea birds are almost all black, white, and gray, so color is less important than flight style and shape. Sure, use your binoculars for a better view of something, but remember, they narrow your field of view and require concentration if you're also trying to hold on (hence, wean yourself of support).

4. DON'T WASTE TIME LOOKING AT DISTANT BIRDS THAT YOU CAN'T IDENTIFY

Most of the species you'll encounter are common, and sooner or later, one will come close to the boat. Then, take a good look, enjoy it (with binoculars!), assimilate it, and then . . .

5. DON'T STOP LOOKING

Watch a Pink-footed Shearwater when it's close and follow it as far as you can see — it will still be a Pink-footed Shearwater long after you can see the field marks you used to identify it when it was close. But slowly you'll absorb nuances that defy articulation, and your pelagic skills will improve steadily.

Oh, and 6. Don't keep reading, get out there on a boat — new frontiers are waiting!

––––––––––––

STEVE HOWELL is a tour leader with the bird-watching company WINGS and a widely published author of books and articles about birds, including the *Peterson Reference Guide to Gulls of the Americas*. He has birded throughout the world's oceans and seen over 90 percent of the world's "true sea birds" — the tubenoses — which are among his favorite birds.

17. *Try the Canadian Great Plains in Winter*
by Paul Kerlinger

B EFORE I FINISHED MY sentence, the look in Ross's
eyes told me I'd put my foot in my mouth. I had
merely stated that the sites I had chosen to study
Snowy Owls were monotonous and that the habitat and topography all looked the same to me. Ross Lein, a biology
professor at the University of Calgary, was raised in southern Saskatchewan and had moved to Boston to attend
Harvard University for his doctoral work. Having been
raised on the prairie, he decided to get even with me:
"While I was at Harvard, I once had to drive down to
Washington, D.C. During that drive it all looked the same
to me." Touché! The prairie Ph.D. knocked me right on
my eastern, suburban ego and made me realize that I
wasn't giving the Great Plains a chance.

That was when I started really thinking about the
northern prairies and realized how interesting they are, especially in winter. What made the biggest impression on
me was my realization that Snowy Owls were regular winter residents. Being from the Northeast, I had rarely seen
Snowies and was under the impression that these birds
were cyclic invaders from the Arctic. The textbooks at that

time had generally portrayed Snowy Owls as Arctic predators that migrate south during years when lemmings are scarce. Crashes in lemming populations were believed to lead to starvation among northern predators, pushing many of these birds southward in search of food. Apparently, this belief was perpetuated mostly among birders from the northeastern United States.

In my first few weeks of cruising the prairies just east of the Rockies, I learned that in Alberta and other parts of the northern Great Plains, Snowy Owls are regular migrants and that they really aren't starving. Ross knew that these birds are regular migrants to Alberta, Saskatchewan, and other parts of the northern Great Plains, and his graduate students were working out the owls' biology. I had the opportunity to be part of that program and learn about Snowy Owls, as well as other aspects of winter prairie birding.

The reason so little is known about Snowy Owl winter populations and biology on the northern Great Plains is undoubtedly the paucity of birders who work those habitats during winter. After all, how long a species list can one accumulate while birding over wheat stubble, grazed pasture, and the small groves of aspen trees that dot the landscape? In three winters, I cruised thousands of miles of gravel and dirt section roads looking for Snowy Owls yet never saw another birder! The fact that Snowy Owls like the seemingly barren wheat stubble, pastures, and other treeless habitats explains why birders hadn't known more about this apparently elusive species.

Spotting Snowy Owls during midday on the prairies really isn't that difficult. Their favorite perch site is on the ground. They seek slightly higher ground or the tops of very subtle rises. On a sunny day, they usually reveal themselves by reflecting sunlight off their breasts, in a brilliant or slightly golden shine. This almost unnatural reflection is a dead giveaway. While I recorded hundreds of sightings, I never saw a Snowy Owl perched in a tree, although I have heard that they do that.

Snowies aren't the only cool birds that make winter prairie birding interesting. The cast of predators is impressive. Early and late in the winter, Rough-legged Hawks are not uncommon. Through the winter I regularly saw Prairie Falcons and Merlins, and on rare occasions, Gyrfalcons, another species that may be more of a regular migrant than a cyclic invader. In addition to these raptors, there were some Golden Eagles, Northern Goshawks, and Short-eared Owls, along with plenty of Bohemian Waxwings, Redpolls, and Gray Partridges.

Perhaps the most oddball phenomenon I witnessed was a gathering of white-tailed jackrabbits. I estimated there were more than two hundred of them. They were congregated in two or three fields in which there was a three-acre copse of aspen trees. The rest of the field was pasture. I quickly learned the meaning of the term "mad as a March hare." These hares were cavorting and interacting for several weeks in February and March. While this gathering of jackrabbits didn't attract birders, predators certainly took note. At one site, I observed two Snowy Owls nearby, one Golden Eagle, a Northern Goshawk, and six coyotes. The raptors were all perched, but the spectacle of those coyotes chasing the rabbits will remain in my memory forever.

I never did see a Snowy Owl pick off a jackrabbit, but I did watch a first-year male Snowy looking down at the rabbits from the top of a thirty-foot-tall power pole. It may have been thinking about the consequences if it bounded to one of the immense rabbits. These rabbits are two to three times heavier than the owls, making the rabbits almost impossible to overpower. The jackrabbits did not seem to be alarmed by the presence of the Snowy, perhaps realizing the small male wasn't a threat. Snowy Owls are known to prey on these rabbits, but it is more likely to be the larger females that do this.

More typical prey of Snowy Owls are the white-footed deer mice that reside mostly in roadside ditches and other patches of unmowed grasses with deep snow cover. This habitat offers relative safety from owls, coyotes, and other predators. In the evening, these mice seek spilled grain in the wheat stubble, where they become more vulnerable. At this time Snowy Owls become more active, moving from perches on or near the ground in the middle of farm fields to roadside fence posts and telephone poles. Birders who observe owls at this time will sometimes be rewarded by witnessing prey capture.

There are good reasons the tour companies don't offer many excursions to the Canadian prairies in the dead of winter. The cold, wind, and a relatively short bird list aren't great attractions for most birders, especially when they could fly to Venezuela and see two hundred species in December or January. Yet Great Plains birding is special and can be addictive. Whereas individual species that make up a long life list sometimes seem to blur, a single sighting of a Snowy Owl or Gyrfalcon can be indelibly etched in one's birding memory. Out there in the seemingly endless wheat fields of Alberta, there are Snowy Owls surviving and thriving in an almost birderless environment.

———————

PAUL KERLINGER cofounded www.CapeMayTimes.com and has authored several books, including *How Birds Migrate* and *The New York City Audubon Society Guide to Finding Birds in the Metropolitan Area*. Previously, he served as director of the Cape May Bird Observatory.

18. Go Birding at Night: The Final Frontier
by Ted Floyd

*D*o *you have any idea what you're getting yourself into?* I'd actually given it some thought.

Everything will change for you. Nothing wrong with a little change of scenery.

You'll never go birding again. Unlikely.

The supposedly life-changing moment took place at 4:22 A.M. on October 4, 2004. That's when Hannah M. Floyd came kicking and screaming (other way around, actually) into the world. Within three hours, she'd gotten her first lifer: a Ring-billed Gull flying past the hospital room right at sunrise. By day's end, Hannah's list was up to fifteen species, among them Black-billed Magpie, Common Raven, and Golden Eagle.

Arguably, nothing had changed. I did as much birding in Hannah's first year of life as in any preceding 365-day interval. Much of the time, I was accompanied by Hannah — out on the rocks at Asilomar Beach (Black Oystercatcher, Wandering Tattler), in Tucson city parks (Gila Woodpecker, Cactus Wren), from the guest room window in Pittsburgh (Swainson's Thrushes passing over on nocturnal migration).

What about those occasions when Hannah was *not* present? What about ordinary birding, with my old birding friends or just by myself? It wouldn't have been very chivalrous of me, I reckoned, to have gone off gallivanting while Hannah was left behind with Mama. But what if the two of them were sleeping? Wouldn't that be okay?

My naysayer friend, it turns out, sort of had a point. Something *did* change. I wound up doing an awful lot of nighttime birding that first year of Hannah's life. I'm not talking about getting up early enough to see the sunrise. Early enough to catch the opening notes of the dawn chorus. No, I'm talking about birding in the dead of night. Just a few owls, right? Throw in a nightjar or two in the summer months, and maybe a rail or night-heron calling from the darkness. And that's it.

Hardly. The nighttime hours, I have found, can be amazingly productive. You can observe more species — and often *many* more individuals of them — than during the day. In many instances, birds at night engage in intriguing behaviors that are rarely detected by day. There is a fascinating psychosensory angle to nighttime birding, too: with fewer distractions in the wee hours of the morning, we are especially attuned to our surroundings. The song of a sparrow in an old pasture is overlooked by day yet bewitching at night. A passing thrush goes unnoticed during the daytime hours, but it is thrilling to watch one transit the disk of the full moon. The Black-bellied Plover's whistled call is plain and simple at noontime, lonely and lovely at midnight.

I'm at the stage now when birding by night is a lot like birding by day was in my earliest years as a birder. Everything is new. Every foray into the darkness promises insight and surprise. I embark upon terra incognita, onto a new frontier of discovery and delight, each time I am out.

Here are some random samples, all from my home state of Colorado:

• *Late May, 3 A.M.* I emerge from my sleeping bag to survey the moonlit sand-sage prairie east of Colorado Springs. I hear a Cassin's Sparrow, then another, and another. At least a dozen of them, singing their melancholy five-part songs. There are Brewer's Sparrows about, too, whose complex songs sound like fishing line being reeled in. A meteor streaks silently past. In the very same instant, an invisible Swainson's Thrush calls — *pweev!* — as it migrates over. Cassin's and Brewer's Sparrows and Swainson's Thrushes are classic LBJs (Little Brown Jobs), but that's beside the point. That's a narrow, *visual* assessment. By night, they are the centerpieces in a haunting soundscape that is not soon forgotten.

• *Mid-June, 2 A.M.* Five friends and I are exploring the foothills of a formation called the Flatirons. Yes, the "conventional" nocturnal species are on hand: five species of owls, two species of nightjars, and a winnowing Wilson's Snipe. But we are just as taken with the many passerine species that are active on this partly cloudy night: Yellow-breasted Chats proclaiming wildly from every thicket, a solitary Grasshopper Sparrow defending his claim to some patch of big bluestem, and Violet-green Swallows twittering above the pines. There is the strange sensation that the night is fleeting and tenuous, yet at the same moment frozen in time.

• *Late September, 6 A.M.* Daybreak comes late in early autumn before the change to standard time, and only the faintest glimmers of dawn are visible from atop the dam at Prewitt Reservoir. There is no dawn chorus yet, and neither will there be one on this cool and cloudy morning. But a friend and I are immersed in bird sound. Behind us, Baird's Sandpipers are in flight; we hear their growling call notes. Ahead of us, passerine migrants are coming in; many of them are Orange-crowned Warblers, but we hear other warbler species, too, along with a few grosbeaks, tanagers, and thrushes. We savor the moment: the new day is aborning, and there will soon be silence.

• *Early April, 9 P.M.* The last vestiges of dusk are no more. It is nighttime now and snowing lightly. Our little group of birders treads silently through the wet meadow. We get too close to a Gadwall, who flushes from a puddle with a disgruntled *kvunk*. A spring of teal follows *(burp . . . burp . . . burp),* and we listen as they pass. It is getting rapidly colder, and only the mellow hooting of a distant Great Horned Owl is audible over the faint hiss of falling snow.

• *Early November, 5 A.M.* My four companions and I are getting our last fix of fall land-bird migration. Most of the birds aloft this overcast night are American Tree Sparrows — the rear guard of the autumn nocturnal migrants. At the same time, the countryside is alive with territorial Great Horned Owls — those first heralds of spring across much of North America.

I am not yet — not by any stretch — an expert at birding by night. There is much more to learn about, much more to discover. And that's the fundamental appeal of night birding: magic and mystery await, every time I am out before first light. I suspect it will always be that way. The great river of nocturnal migration, the drama of nighttime courtship displays, the soft banter of a pair of distant owls — these things will forever remain invisible, literally so, challengingly and alluringly so. Nighttime birding presents one of the ultimate challenges for the modern birder, but it also reconnects us with that unforgotten sense of wonder from our earliest years.

TED FLOYD is the editor of *Birding,* the flagship publication of the American Birding Association. He has published more than one hundred articles in professional journals and popular magazines and is the author of several forthcoming books on birds.

19. *Birder or Bird Watcher? You Decide*
by Scott Shalaway

I F YOU'RE READING THIS book, you probably enjoy seeing birds in your backyard. You may not consider yourself a birder or even a bird watcher, but you appreciate the sights and sounds wild birds provide.

Though my dictionary doesn't distinguish between the terms *bird watcher* and *birder,* I do. In my mind, a bird watcher is more casual about the pastime and concentrates on backyard birds. A birder tends to be more obsessed. He devotes most of his spare time to watching birds and often plans vacations and even business trips around birding hot spots. And most birders keep a life list — a list of all the species seen since the obsession began.

I consider myself both a bird watcher and a birder. In my twenties and thirties, I was more birder. I competed with friends on bird counts and Big Days (twenty-four-hour competitions to see who could record the most species). I even led birding tours to Mexico in the late 1980s. But raising a family changes one's priorities. A parent must also focus on the passions of his children and his spouse. So my days of wild-goose chases became fewer and more precious.

Occasionally, the obsession creeps back into my life. During the last week of April 2003, West Virginia hosted the first annual New River Birding and Nature Festival, and I was invited to speak. I jumped at the chance because it would put me in Swainson's Warbler country just as these elusive birds were returning to the northern limits of their breeding grounds. I had never seen a Swainson's Warbler, so this was my big chance. Dave Pollard, the organizer of the festival, promised to get me to Swainson's habitat, but he did his best to dampen my optimism about seeing the bird.

"I can almost guarantee you'll hear the bird, but it's tough to see," he warned. "It hides itself well in the dense rhododendron thickets."

"If I hear it," I replied, "I'll see it." Cockier words were never spoken.

At first light the day after my presentations, a group was to assemble at the Fern Creek parking area, not far from the Canyon Rim visitors' center at New River Gorge. Swainson's had been heard there the day before. As I drove to the meeting place, I listened to a recording of the Swainson's song — a series of loud slurred whistles with an emphatic ending.

When I arrived at the parking area, the first sound I heard was a series of loud slurred whistles with an emphatic ending. Getting a life bird had never been so easy.

The group listened intently for ten minutes as the Swainson's Warbler sang every twenty to thirty seconds. It stayed hidden about thirty yards away in a rhododendron thicket.

We then moved on to bird other areas of the gorge. I was thrilled to have heard a new bird but disappointed that I hadn't seen it. I have a rule that, to count a new bird on my life list, I've got to see it well enough to identify it by sight. This small, drab brown bird with a rusty cap and dark eye line was proving as elusive as I'd been promised.

Later that morning I left the group and returned to the Fern Creek parking lot. The bird was still singing from the same spot where we had heard it hours earlier. I walked quietly a short distance toward the sound until I reached the creek. The bird couldn't have been more than fifteen yards away, but it remained undetectable in the dense thicket.

I sat and listened for thirty minutes while the bird sang, but it never moved. I pished and squeaked and pulled in a cardinal, an Ovenbird, a Worm-eating Warbler, and several Black-throated Green Warblers, which perched nervously on a branch not ten feet away.

Finally, after more than an hour, I caught a glimpse of a small, dark bird darting through the thicket. I pished, I squeaked. I even whistled like a screech-owl to trigger its defensive curiosity. Finally the bird popped into view. My heart quickened as I raised my binoculars. Then it sank — just another Ovenbird.

Three years and three more trips to the New River Gorge later, and I still haven't checked Swainson's Warbler on my life list. But if every bird were easy to see, there'd be no challenge.

And it's the challenge to see the unseeable that makes birding so appealing. Anyone can see common birds, and even rare birds can be easy to see if you're in the right place at the right time. It's the elusive species that can take years to find that make birding the most obsessive and addictive habit I know.

But birding is much more than seeing rare or new birds and checking them on a list. Whether birder, bird watcher, or just casual bird lover, anyone can appreciate wild birds. A flock of cardinals in a snowstorm, a chorus of Wood Thrushes at sunrise in May, a cloud of hummingbirds at a back porch feeder on an August evening; these common sights and sounds from my own backyard thrill me as much as seeing a new life bird.

SCOTT SHALAWAY writes a weekly syndicated column for newspapers, hosts two weekly radio shows, teaches Ornithology for Teachers at Ohio State University's Stone Laboratory, and is the author of *Building a Backyard Bird Habitat*.

20. *Linger Even After You've Listed a Bird*
by John Sill

CATHY AND I WERE both fortunate to have been raised in families that enjoyed nature and introduced us to its wonders. Though I was a bit more focused on birds than Cathy was, both of her parents were bona fide bird watchers. So when she married me, a bird artist, she moved easily into the world of watching birds. We soon became aware of a new emphasis in bird watching: the list. We both knew the birds we had seen, but now everyone was counting theirs. And former bird watchers had now become birders.

As an aspiring artist trying to get established, I decided I needed at least four hundred birds on my North American life list in order to be credible, so we went from simply watching birds to checking them off our lists. We traveled on a fairly tight schedule in those years. This didn't allow a great deal of time to just sit and soak up a bird. Besides, we were intent on adding to our lists. While we were spotting birds, I wasn't really *seeing* birds. My list was growing, but my art wasn't benefiting from seeking new birds. After some years of this, we passed four hundred, then five hundred, and the chase was losing its joy.

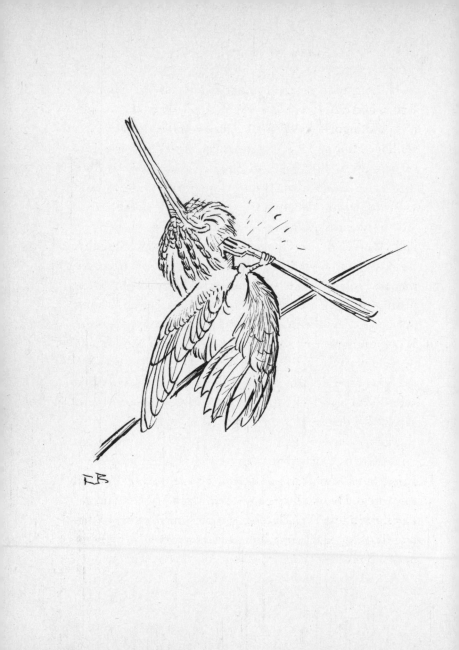

Then one typically wonderful day at the Spofford Ranch in Arizona we were watching the show. As myriads of hummingbirds and their kin came and went, we saw a Calliope Hummingbird above us in a big oak. He was only our second, and this was by far our best view. We watched the bird preen. He dropped his wing, turned his head, and scratched his ear. What a moment! Cathy then decided to start a "scratching-its-ear" list.

From this smallest of North American hummingbirds we realized that we had been missing the great opportunity we birders have to witness particular moments in the life of a bird. Joy rediscovered. Any list can be fun and can provide a kind of diary of birds and places and situations. What our "scratching-its-ear" list has done for us is cause us to linger with birds. Though we do keep records and mark birds seen, we could only ballpark our life lists if you asked. Pick a behavior and make a list if you like, but if at all possible, linger with birds.

———————

JOHN SILL has been a wildlife artist specializing in birds since 1970. His work has appeared in a number of magazines, including *Bird Watcher's Digest*, *Birder's World*, *Natural History*, and *Birding*. Sill's paintings have been exhibited in *Birds in Art* and *Art of the Animal Kingdom*.

21. *Shift Your Focus from Birding to Birds*
by Kevin J. Cook

B
IRDING IS LIKE EATING a fine meal.

The first hundred life birds are the appetizer, each lifer a delicious bite that prepares your palate for more good things to come. The second hundred are the salad, each lifer fresh and crisp and exciting. The third hundred are the soup, each lifer a bit of cheese in the French onion broth. The fourth hundred are the bread, each lifer a warm slice that gratifies. The fifth hundred are a veggie medley, each lifer piquant in its own way. The sixth hundred are the entrée, each lifer a bite-by-bite delight unto itself. The seventh hundred are the dessert, each lifer a sheer pleasure. The eighth hundred are the after-dinner drink, each lifer a delicate swallow of fine liqueur or wine or coffee.

And then reality happens: the meal ends.

Truth be told, for many of us, birding is less like fine dining and more like endless grazing at the fast-food place down the street; but the point of the metaphor is the inevitable question of what to do when the meal ends. As your birding life progresses, life birds become fewer and farther between. And then what? Does birding end when the life listing is done?

Some people simply divert their birding energy to new listing games: year lists, state lists, county lists, Tuesday lists. Some people extend their birding energy to the international scene: Belize, Costa Rica, Australia.

But acknowledging that reality thing, a lot of us live behind doors on which Opportunity never knocks, and for us, the kiwis of New Zealand, the babblers of Africa, and the bustards of Asia will forever remain exotic.

So what do you do with your birding when life listing slows from a torrent to a trickle to a drip, when year listing becomes more chore than pleasure, when international birding is limited to crossing the state line? What comes next? Shift your focus from birding to birds!

Rather than pursuing goals such as how many species you can see in a day or chasing after the latest rarity, set goals of seeing things you've never seen on birds that you have seen.

Have you seen the booted tarsus on an American Robin, a trait it shares with bluebirds, thrushes, and solitaires? Have you seen the perforate nostril on a Turkey Vulture, a trait that it shares with condors but that is absent from hawks and eagles?

Surely you've seen Great Horned Owls and House

Sparrows, but have you seen a House Sparrow snuggle a light bulb to stay warm on a frigid winter night? Or watched a Great Horned Owl actually hunt and egest one of those famous pellets?

Have you experienced these things by deliberate effort or by serendipity? Do you even know what a tarsus is, let alone a booted one? How about a perforate nostril?

Not everything birdy is in a field guide.

Before 1934, credible bird identification required fundamental ornithological knowledge. Roger Tory Peterson's remarkable innovation of field guides changed that by allowing a person to identify birds without having to learn about birds. And millions of people have.

But if we take the food metaphor seriously, birding is not so much like eating a fine meal as it is like stuffing down hot, yummy bread sticks and never tasting the lasagna.

Shifting your focus from birding to birds engages the personal process of knowledge acquisition. Most birders learn something about birds, but tidbits of disjointed factual information do not equate to knowledge. When you focus on the bird, you realize that, more than just a group of individuals that can produce offspring, a species is an expression of life, a way of living, and as such, each species bears a story. And all the stories of all the species interweave to form the fabric of life on Earth.

Hummingbirds don't just visit flowers; they are pollinators, agents of sex by courier. Waxwings don't just swallow fruits; they disperse seeds. Nutcrackers don't just cache pine seeds; they plant forests.

When your birding winds down, focus on the birds that you know, and learn how they live and how they die. Birding leads to avian awareness; avian awareness, given the chance, can lead to ornithological literacy.

If you think adding a bird to your life list is fun, wait until you discover the thrill of coming to know a bird! Flammulated Owls, for example, are so seriously cute they make kittens look ugly; but seeing the owl is not the same as knowing the owl. Knowing the Flammulated Owl requires understanding quaking aspen, ponderosa pine, Douglas fir, Red-naped Sapsuckers, snowy tree-crickets, and the moths called millers that develop from caterpillars called army cutworms.

Knowing that such a thing as the Flammulated Owl exists is avian awareness; understanding how insects and trees and sapsuckers collectively influence the way Flammulated Owls live and die is ornithological literacy. The personal rewards of each are legion.

To use the food metaphor a final time, birding is a bag of French fries, but birds themselves are a great banquet, and learning about birds is like feasting at that banquet.

KEVIN J. COOK has worked as a writer-naturalist since 1975. Besides writing, he conducts seminars, classes, and tours, all based on wildlife themes. His credo "Birds do not live alone!" fires his passion for the connectedness between birds and the rest of the living world.

22. *Don't Forget to Listen*
by Louise Zemaitis

A TOUR PARTICIPANT RECENTLY asked me what some of my favorite birding spots were. I gave it some thought. I imagined myself standing on the Alaskan tundra hearing nothing but the winnowing of Wilson's Snipes; awakening before dawn in the Belizean rainforest to the first songs of Montezuma Oropendolas at their nests with the roars of howler monkeys in the distance; and standing at Cape May Point, wrapped in misty darkness, as the sky above is filled with bird sound from nocturnal migrants making contact with one another. It was then that I realized how important sound has become to me.

For the beginner, birding is mostly a visual endeavor. Size, structure, and behavior are the primary things that a birder must consider when identifying birds. But I think that learning bird sound shouldn't wait. The younger we are when we learn sounds, the better. Children pick up language far more quickly than adults do. I've always suspected that my husband, Michael O'Brien, has had an edge over all of us because he learned birdsong seemingly from birth. His father and brother are also birders, and their

family home is in a woodland oasis. Michael started night listening when he was a paperboy.

When you find a bird, don't just look at it and walk away. Continue to study it. Listen to all of the sounds that it makes. Learning bird sounds may seem like a daunting task. Take it on progressively. Just think: if you learn three warbler songs each year, in just ten years you've got most of them.

As you learn, expand upon what you know. It's like building a vocabulary. But it won't work unless it makes sense to you. Does a Tufted Titmouse sound like it says *chiva chiva chiva*? Or is it more like *peter peter peter*? Swainson's Warblers are notoriously hard to see. Do you listen for *here here here we go* or *ooh ooh stepped in poo*? I think that the latter is much more memorable. Use whatever tricks work for you. I'll always remember that Short-billed Dowitchers say *tututu* because Dick Walton (author of the Birding by Ear CDs) ordered a "Short-billed Dowitcher" for breakfast at a restaurant in Cape May one morning. He proceeded to tell the puzzled waitress that it meant two eggs, two pancakes, and two pieces of bacon.

Having a musical ear helps. I've noticed that birders who love music are more interested in bird sound. It is an awesome event when tour leaders have a jam session or attend a local karaoke night during birding festivals. We all have more musical knowledge than we realize. Just think of all those lyrics that you learned in your youth. They're still in there! I would gladly trade the words to any disco song for a few more tropical birdcalls.

Even though you may have picked up birding after your youth, it's never too late to start learning birdsong. If listening to the CDs on which the birdsong immediately follows an announcement of its name launches you into a nice daydream, then try a tutorial such as Birding by Ear. I must admit that I found tutorials more to my liking when I was starting out.

Find a mentor. As much as I love bird books and CDs, there's nothing like learning from an old sage. Or in my case, a rising star. Michael and other leaders like him are eager to share their knowledge. Don't be afraid to ask questions. Attend birding field trips and workshops. They will greatly reduce your learning curve.

Do a Big Day. It may feel a little like baptism by fire, but it is an amazing learning experience. Going through a twenty-four-hour period using sound as well as sight for identifying birds by species will force you to learn more quickly, for several reasons, not the least of which is pride. You certainly want to keep up with your teammates and not be the weak link. And it really is fun. Then, when you do finally lay your head upon your pillow at the end of the day, you will continue to hear the sounds of the birds in your head as you drift off to sleep.

Natural sounds are a joy. All of my favorite memories include them and would instantly be diminished with the introduction of man-made noise. I know that we can create a kind of filter for the sounds of airplanes and automobiles, but when you visit a place without them you will notice the difference. Do your best to get outside and enjoy the natural world — and don't forget to listen.

LOUISE ZEMAITIS is an artist, naturalist, and WINGS tour leader living in Cape May, New Jersey. She is a popular field-trip leader in Cape May, where she leads bird and butterfly walks and teaches birding workshops as an associate naturalist with the Cape May Bird Observatory. Zemaitis is also coordinator of the Monarch Monitoring Project in Cape May and curator of the Cape May Bird Observatory art gallery. An honors graduate of Temple University's Tyler School of Art, she enjoys working as a freelance artist, and her illustrations have been widely published.

23. *Go Beyond Identifying Birds to Identifying* with *Them*

by Donald Kroodsma

SONG SPARROW. SOMEWHERE in my subconscious, the well-honed detectors fire. It's the familiar quality and rhythm, some buzzes, some nice whistles, three to five distinct parts to the song, beginning with an accelerating series of notes and ending with a low buzz. One song is all it takes, because there's nothing else quite like it.

I now stop, fully conscious. Who is this bird? What's on his mind? I listen to his next song, feeling the overall quality and rhythm and declaring it the same as or different from his first. And I listen to the next song, and the next. If he keeps singing, I know that eventually he will change his tune, that he will go on to sing a series of a strikingly different song, a song so different that anyone who pays attention will hear it. He has, after all, eight to ten different songs, and if I just keep listening, I know I'll hear him switch.

How many songs of each type does he sing before he switches? Inevitably, I count, as a way of paying my respects. If he's an old friend, I take notes so I can compare his mood from day to day. In the excitement of dawn singing, for example, I know he'll repeat a given song relatively few times before switching to another, but during more leisurely singing later in the day, he switches less frequently.

I might sketch his songs, too, so that I get to know each of them; I use my experience with sonagrams, but almost any crude stick figure that captures the essence of the song will do. Which particular song is he singing now? Which of his other songs is most likely to follow? Does he have favorites?

This sparrow is also part of a community, and I listen to what the other Song Sparrows are doing nearby. Are they singing? If so, is there any evidence that they're paying attention to one another? Do they rather politely take turns singing? Or does one rudely overlap the songs of another? Maybe they switch songs together? If so, do they switch to especially similar or especially different songs?

Other birds sing like this, too, delivering a series of one song before switching to another. Their singing habits allow for leisurely listening, as the songs and switches come at a pace that I can easily keep up with. I especially enjoy listening to titmice, cardinals, and several wrens in this way.

Other species have different singing games. In some species, singers are known to have just one song, so I listen to a series of songs just to confirm that successive songs are all the same. White-throated and Chipping Sparrows are good examples, as are Ovenbirds. With a Black-capped Chickadee, I want to hear if he sings the widespread *hey-sweetie* song, listening closely to hear that brief pause in the middle of the *sweetie*. And if he keeps singing, I wait until he raises or lowers the pitch of his song, because all good chickadees sing a series of *hey-sweetie*s on one pitch before leaping to another.

With some other species, the game is far more challenging for me. Take a mockingbird, for example. From various studies, I know he has anywhere from 100 to 150 songs that he can sing. As he sings, I listen to how he switches to a new song every second or two, but I listen mostly for an especially distinctive song that I know I'll recognize when he returns to sing it again. Every bird, even a mockingbird, has a handle by which I can get to know him, and I listen until I find that handle. If he continues to sing, I listen, waiting for my chosen song to occur again. Eureka! There it is. Now more certain, I might start counting, wondering how many different songs he will deliver before returning to the song I recognize. How far I count tells me roughly how many different songs he can sing.

Or take a Wood Thrush, one of the finest singers on the planet. I hear three parts to the song, soft initial *bup bup bup* notes followed by rich whistled notes (what I call the "prelude") and then a rapidly delivered, almost percussive trill (the "flourish"). The *bup*s are always the same, but he combines his preludes and flourishes so that successive songs are always different. As he sings, I pick out his most distinctive prelude and listen for him to sing it again. How many other preludes intervene before he repeats it? I might sketch that prelude, then pick out the next most distinctive one, and the next, until I have mastered his repertoire of two to eight different preludes. Perhaps I'll keep track of a longer series of songs, writing down in my notebook how he works through his preludes. I might tackle some of the flourishes, too, because some of them are sufficiently distinctive, but many sound too similar to one another for my ears to distinguish.

And how exhilarating to truly listen to a western Marsh Wren or Sage Thrasher or Brown Thrasher or Hermit Thrush or Red-eyed Vireo or the most common of birds, the American Robin. Each species plays its own singing games, and as they sing, I listen, trying to understand what they're up to, trying to use their singing as a window on their minds. When encountering new birds or especially when traveling to new places, I'm more eager to *identify with* a particular singing bird than I am to *identify* it, as truly listening does not require that I first label the songster.

"Oh, sure, you can do all that, but I can't because . . ." I have a suggestion for the doubter. Next time you hear a singing bird that intrigues you, sit down and get comfortable, take out pencil and paper, and listen, writing down twenty questions that come to mind. Big questions, little questions, serious ones, silly ones, it matters not, but aim for twenty. Then look them over. You'll realize that answering some of them would take a lifetime, but others you will answer with just a little attentive listening. That small exercise will start you on listening adventures you never thought possible.

DONALD KROODSMA won the 2006 John Burroughs Medal for his book *The Singing Life of Birds*. He is professor emeritus at the University of Massachusetts, has studied birdsong for more than thirty years, and was recognized as the "reigning authority on the biology of avian vocal behavior" in the citation for his 2003 Elliot Coues Award from the American Ornithologists' Union.

24. Don't Play with Firecrackers: Where Have All the Birdsongs Gone?
by Lang Elliott

I AM A PROFESSIONAL nature recordist, specializing in the songs and calls of birds. This may not seem odd, but it is. Why? Because I have severe high-frequency deafness and cannot hear even half of the sounds that birds make. I am able to do my work only because I have a device that takes the high-pitched sounds I cannot hear and lowers them into a range where my hearing is still, fortunately, okay.

I damaged my hearing by playing with firecrackers when I was a kid. It was well before I gained a healthy respect for my hearing and before my fascination with nature led to a heartfelt aversion to hurting living things.

So here's the ugly truth.

My friend Skip and I were attempting to blow up a squirrel's nest high in an oak tree. We had an ample supply of "cherry bomb" firecrackers, those obnoxious red noisemakers that look like cherries with fuses. We'd light one, watch the fuse burn down, and then fling the cherry bomb at the nest, hoping it would explode at just the right time.

We didn't know for sure if the nest was occupied, but we certainly intended to find out.

But our plan backfired, quite literally.

While I was fumbling around trying to fish another cherry bomb out of my pocket, Skip tossed one up. But it hit a low limb and bounced directly back at us. Skip jumped out of the way, yelling "watch out," but I didn't even have time to look up. The cherry bomb exploded an inch or two above me, singeing the top of my head and blasting my ears with such intense sound that gobs of nerves in my cochleae — those very nerves that respond to high-pitched sounds, including the songs of birds — were fried in an instant.

I curse the fact that my eardrums were so strong. Had they simply ruptured, the nerves in my inner ears may have been protected, and I might have regained most of my hearing. After the blast, my sound world disappeared entirely. All I could hear for a day or two was ringing in my ears. I could see people moving their lips, but I heard no sound. My hearing gradually returned. Within a week I was as good as new, or at least I thought I was. I could once again hear my friends speak, and I went about my daily business as if nothing had happened.

Everything seemed normal, except for minor little annoyances, such as dropping a dime on the sidewalk and not hearing it *ping*. Or not hearing the subtle hiss of air escaping from my bicycle tire, or the whistling of a teakettle when the water was boiling. Okay, I can live with that, I thought, but I had no idea those sounds were all high-pitched, and along with not hearing them I was not hearing the lovely sounds of warblers, waxwings, creepers, and all those insects that trill and scrape as summer turns to fall. I didn't make that connection until years later.

As a young man, I was a graduate student at the University of Maryland, taking a course in animal behavior taught by the ornithologist Eugene S. Morton, of the National Zoo. On one occasion, I visited his house along the Severn River near Annapolis, and the two of us went for a long walk. As we approached a wooded hillside, Gene became very excited when he heard the trill of a Worm-eating Warbler, a rarity in his area. I didn't hear a thing. So Gene led me to the very tree in which it was singing. We stood beneath the tree, no more than twenty feet from the little singer, whose trill was enormously loud at that point. I still didn't hear a thing.

Gene encouraged me to get my hearing tested, which I did in short measure. To my dismay, I learned I was severely deaf at frequencies of four thousand cycles per second (four kilohertz) and above. I could still hear spring peepers cheeping away at three kilohertz, but I couldn't hear a phoebe or a wood-pewee singing at four kilohertz, no matter how close I got. And I couldn't hear all those warblers singing from four to eight kilohertz and above. And the high calls of Cedar Waxwings, Brown Creepers, and Brown-headed Cowbirds? Why, they no longer existed in my world of sound. I had imagined myself being a hear-all, see-all naturalist, perfectly tuned in to the natural world. And now I had learned the hard truth: I couldn't hear half of what was going on out there. What an absolute bummer.

But I was resilient. I knew that there is more to life than good hearing, and I certainly wouldn't be so foolish as to try to make a living recording those very sounds that I couldn't hear. Or at least you'd think I wouldn't be so foolish . . .

But here I am, many years later, doing just that. It really makes no sense at all. If anything, my hearing has worsened. I can't hear those peepers nearly as well as I used to. But I've learned to live with it. And, as I said in the beginning, I found a way around it all. I developed a device that lets me hear those high-pitched birds. Not as well as someone with normal hearing, but well enough, I suppose, to do the work I do.

These days, getting good recordings is actually very easy. I do it by wandering around in nature, waiting for the singers to come to me and peck me squarely on the head, demanding that I record them as they perch above me on a low limb. They tell me that the squirrels have forgiven me, and they are here to bring me their blessings. And then they sing their hearts out just over my head, not far above where the cherry bomb once exploded my ears away.

———————

LANG ELLIOTT is the owner of NatureSound Studio and has produced numerous books and audio guides to the sounds of birds, frogs, insects, and mammals, including *Common Birds and Their Songs* and *The Songs of Wild Birds.* He is also the coinventor of The SongFinder, a digital birdsong listening device.

25. *Become a Pod Person: The iBirder*
by Noah Strycker

Y OU SEE THEM EVERYWHERE. Field marks include glazed eyes, sweatshirt hoods pulled forward, baggy pants, and a perpetual shuffling gait. The distinguishing characteristic is a curious white wire running from each ear down to waist level. These are the Pod People. I know because I am one — of the friendly *iBirder* subspecies, but more on that in a minute.

The iPod portable digital player, made by Apple, has become so intertwined with my college age bracket that we are increasingly being called the "iPod Generation." This little white box, smaller than a deck of cards, releases a steady stream of personalized musical bliss directly into the ears — innocuous enough at face value but alarming to social critics who warn that young people today have become too solipsistic and isolated. Whatever the social implications, the iPod has become a movement of its own, with runaway sales and little white earphones to mark the era of plugged-in-and-tuned-out Pod People.

Well, sort of. I listen to music on my iPod, but I believe it also has a higher purpose. Which is to say, I've discovered the iPod is great for birding. That little gizmo more than proved its worth one spring morning in an impressive demonstration in a patch of ponderosa pine forest. I decided which songbird I wanted to see, dialed up the pre-programmed call on my iPod, broadcast the song through an external speaker, and — *bada bing!* — there it was, a male Chipping Sparrow, hormones pumping, singing madly from the branch in front of me. In less than ten seconds, I dialed up another species, and the process repeated itself. Like magic. Dial-A-Bird.

In truth, iBirding is far from magic, actually more of a procedure. You have to know exactly where the birds are and when they'll be there. Knowledge of vocalizations helps immensely, since birds heard at a distance can be called in that way. You should be able to differentiate between an actual warbler song and a recording broadcast by the guy across the way with his own iPod. Occasionally, though, luck is all it takes.

On another occasion, it was near midnight and I was standing alone in the inky blackness of an Oregon night. Large tree trunks loomed, framed by the full moon behind dark clouds, on either side of the remote logging road. A creepy silence blanketed the scene. I had a tip that Barred Owls were in the area, and I wanted to see one. In the past ten minutes, however, nothing had stirred. It was time for Plan B. I dialed up "Barred Owl" on my trusty iPod and played the recording, a raucous *whoo-cooks-for-you-all,* twice. Silence. The silence intensified, strangling everything in its grip. Suddenly, a loud *swoosh* sliced the air above my head — then more silence. The hair on the back of my neck prickled. I reached for a flashlight. Owling isn't for the superstitious, that's for sure. Finally, a small noise above my head led me to aim the light and find the owl sitting not five feet from my hat, staring down with somber, watery black eyes — windows to the underworld. I was out of there in a snap and home to bed before it could blink.

In case your handheld speaker isn't loud enough (mine is plenty loud), I've perfected another technique of iBirding that works best when owling. Use your sound system on wheels — the car stereo. Simply hook up the iPod to the car player (sometimes this can be tricky, because you need either an FM transmitter to sync it with your radio or a special connector cable), then drive to the owling spot. When you reach your destination, *do not exit the vehicle*. The owls might see you and fly away. Open the doors, recline your seat, and crank the owl call through those car speakers. With this method, I once drove right up to a barn, aimed the headlights, played the call, and watched a Barn Owl fly out and circle overhead before returning to the barn.

If this isn't extreme birding, I don't know what is.

As a tool for modern birders, the iPod is both handy and reasonably inexpensive, $100 to $450, depending on the model and accessories. It goes with your state-of-the-art binoculars, spotting scope, digital camera, long camera lenses, cell phone with preprogrammed Rare Bird Alert numbers, tuna sandwiches, and BRD BOY license plates. (You can get everything but the plates — those are mine, sorry.) On a nice, leisurely walk around the neighborhood, I'm packing at least fifty pounds of gear. When that rarity appears, I'm ready to (1) call it in with my iPod, (2) look at it, (3) look at it better, (4) photograph it, (5) phone in the alert, and (6) eat lunch.

These days, being properly equipped is half the battle in birding. The iPod helps. Don't expect an iPod to make you an elite birder, though. It can't replace actual knowledge and experience, and it takes a fair amount of time to set up. The setup is managed from a free computer program called iTunes, within which you can download bird recordings and organize the sound files into playlists for field use, both for broadcast and for reference. On outings, I follow common sense with my iPod, trying to be unobtrusive and considerate of birds' activities, especially in heavily birded areas, and never using playbacks for attracting any species that is threatened, endangered, or of special concern.

Pod People do spend a lot of time floating in their own iPod sea. But as a birding tool, the iPod can also be a great way to reach out to the world around us. And that's cool, not just for the iPod Generation but for any generation.

NOAH STRYCKER (birdboy@bkpix.com) is associate editor of *Birding* magazine. Strycker studies fisheries and wildlife science and art at Oregon State University. He received a prestigious 2006 Udall Scholarship and was named ABA/Leica 2004 Young Birder of the Year. His bird photographs, artwork, and articles have appeared in regional and national publications.

26. *Shush and Pish*

by Julie Craves

ANYONE WHO HAS SPENT an appreciable amount of time watching birds knows that it can be frustrating getting a good look. That's why most experienced birders are able to recognize many species not only when they see them but also when they hear them.

But what about those silent birds, the ones you know are there because you catch a glimpse in the undergrowth? Perhaps a bit of wing here, a glance of tail there, a glimmer of a taunting eyeball. If after some patient maneuvering I don't gain a view, I give the bird a little pish.

Pishing is an acoustic method used to lure birds out of hiding. Some purists would say pishing refers only to a single, particular sound, but most people think of pishing as a collective term for a bunch of noises that somehow tempt birds to expose themselves. In basic form, pishing involves clenching the front teeth and quickly saying the word *pish,* quietly but urgently. A variation might be keeping your teeth clenched and saying *seet* in a hissing manner. Alternatively, a squeaking sound can be made by kissing the tip of your finger or back of your hand with tightly pursed lips. Clicking your tongue adds another flourish.

One or the other or some combination of these sounds usually causes the skulking bird to pop into view to investigate the source of the hullabaloo. Some species respond more readily than others. Chickadees, sparrows, and wrens react quickly to pishing, being generally nosy to begin with. If you have mastered the technique, it can be effective enough to bring in a whole bunch of birds that were lurking in the vicinity, as if by magic. Staying still, pishing close to cover where birds will feel comfortable showing themselves, and persistence are all keys to pishing success.

Nobody is quite sure exactly why pishing is such an effective bird-attracting tactic. The best explanation is that it evokes some sort of mobbing behavior, wherein small gangs of birds respond to a predator by excitedly gathering around and trying to outnumber and confuse it while calling in reinforcements. If you have ever witnessed a hectic swarm of incensed little birds harassing an owl, you will have heard an assortment of sounds similar to those that pishing aims to imitate.

Humans also react to pishing. When you're with other birders, you can make these unusual sounds without anybody raising an eyebrow. I've pished in the company of kindred souls all over the United States, as well as in Mexico, Germany, Panama, and even Cuba, and the reaction from my companions was no different than had I coughed. Pish around nonbirders, who have no idea what you are doing, however, and the response may be the same as if you had made some other type of bodily noise. Thus, I recommend being judicious with your pishing.

Embarrassing social situations aside, birds do get used to it. During any given pishing event, they will lose interest after only a few minutes. Pish the same birds frequently, and they'll ignore you as a phony provocateur. I don't pish near nesting birds, if there are predators around, or if it's really cold. Pishing is, after all, evocative, perhaps alarming, to the birds, distracting them from their normal routines. Birding is about enjoying birds as they go about their business. If you're patient, birds will nearly always show themselves. But every so often, if a really reluctant bird needs just a bit of coaxing, you might find that a little pish will do ya.

JULIE CRAVES is the supervisor of avian research for the Rouge River Bird Observatory at the University of Michigan, Dearborn. She is also a contributing editor to *Birder's World* magazine, an author, and a freelance science writer.

Mind Your Manners

27. *Oh, Behave!*
by Mel White

YOU'RE AT A POPULAR birding spot on a May morning when you meet another binocular toter on the trail. "Seen anything good?" you ask.

With a big smile on her face, the other birder says, "I just saw my first Chestnut-sided Warbler! It was so beautiful!"

Your response is to

(a) frown and say, "I can't believe you've never seen Chestnut-sided Warbler before."

(b) shrug and say, "I had three of them already this morning. They're singing all over the place."

(c) laugh and say, "I asked if you'd seen anything *good*."

And the answer is . . . that I sincerely hope you recognized this as a joke. Because if you didn't, congratulations: the new birders you've discouraged over the years quite possibly rival the total on your life list. A number, by the way, I'm sure you'd be happy to share with me.

The correct response to someone else's happy sighting does not begin with "I" — unless the next words are "think that's great!"

Competitiveness in birding can be a good thing, contributing to our sport's fun and its value. The urge to join friends and set a new record for your local Christmas Bird Count adds a challenge to the event and promotes better coverage of the count circle. There's nothing wrong with wanting to have the biggest Big Day in your state, or the highest list for your county. It's the element of birding one-upmanship that's distressing and, I believe, dispiriting to many beginners.

Admit it. If you've been a birder for a few years, you've heard an exchange like this more times than you like to recall:

"We went to Costa Rica last month. What a fabulous place! We saw three hundred and forty species in a week."

"Yeah, we went there in 'ninety-nine. Had four hundred and thirty-six species. We were the first people to find a Double-spotted Mudrunner in Guanacaste Province since the eighteenth century."

Really, wouldn't a nicer response have been "That sounds terrific. What were your favorite birds?"

Am I being overly Pollyanna-ish here? I don't think so.

When someone says, "Our daughter is getting married next month," the typical reaction is "Congratulations." It's not "Oh, we've had two daughters get married, both at Gilded Lily Country Club. The first one married a heart surgeon, the second one married a Greek shipping heir.

We spent more than a hundred and fifty thousand dollars both times." Yet there seems to be something about the birding psyche that, too often, brings on just that sort of exchange.

Do I have a completely pure heart? Not at all — I recognize myself on both sides of these conversations. To be charitable to myself and to others, birding is so often a solitary undertaking that we all walk around with pent-up urges to share our sightings. We were alone when we got that superb look at a Calliope Hummingbird, so when someone else mentions the bird, our "Me, too" pops out before we even think about it.

It's true, though, that there are birders I avoid, because I know no matter what subject comes up, they'll make sure I know that they've seen more birds than I have, seen better birds than I have, and been to more interesting places than I have — and what's more, they know the molt sequences of shorebird wing feathers better than I do.

I suppose there's some justification for the ABC Bird Tour Company claiming that its trip to Belize sees more birds than the trip run by the XYZ Bird Tour Company. Pepsi claims it tastes better than Coke. It's business. But for most of us, birding is a hobby. It's supposed to be fun.

If you want to arm-wrestle, go on down to the biker bar and leave the rest of us to enjoy the Chestnut-sided Warblers.

MEL WHITE is a freelance writer who lives in Little Rock, Arkansas, and specializes in travel and natural history. He's especially grateful to the publications that have sent him to interesting places where he's been able to watch birds in between work duties.

28. *Heed Birding's Traditions and Taboos*

by Wayne R. Petersen

A S A BIRDER WITH HALF a century of experience behind me, I deem myself qualified to comment on a
few realities of birding etiquette. Since birding is a
culture steeped in traditions and taboos, ethics and values,
these key guidelines may help a new birder better negotiate
those embarrassing or politically incorrect circumstances
that inevitably arise whenever birders get together. The
immediate or long-term repercussions of ignoring these
guidelines cannot be overstated. All are more or less central
to birding culture and consequently deserve thoughtful
consideration.

- Never ask: "What's the total of your list?" This topic is
  a minefield, and understanding the sensitivity of it is
  essential to maintaining positive birding relationships,
  especially when encountering an unknown birder for
  the first time. While some birders readily tout their list
  totals (life list, American Birding Association area list,
  state list, county list, et cetera), others are covetous of
  this information. Whether for reasons of pride, self-
  consciousness, or plain old-fashioned humility, many

birders don't wish to be confronted with this most personal of birding questions. Use discretion!

- A second question never to ask is, "Are you sure about the identification of that bird?" To some birders, such a query amounts to a full frontal assault. Indeed, more feelings are hurt, friendships broken, and egos destroyed by this question than by practically any other in the birding culture. To avoid running amuck of this taboo, simply *consider carefully before asking*. Because this question inherently challenges a birder's integrity and competence, full awareness of its ramifications is in order. The point is not avoiding the question but rather considering how to ask it. There is no panacea for this prickly issue, other than to remain cognizant of how *you* wish to be treated when your competence or veracity is brought into question. Harmonious resolution of this dilemma lies more in process than in outcome.

- Sharing is central to birding etiquette. What birder has never been the beneficiary of the generosity provided by another? Generosity ranges from freely disseminating information about the presence of an unusual bird to offering directions to a visiting birder or providing identification assistance with an unfamiliar species. The ethic of sharing information, although not endemic to the birding culture, is a virtue all too often lacking in other routine endeavors. Birders willing to share information and knowledge will never be out of step with birding etiquette.

- Strict adherence to the principles of honesty and integrity is intrinsic to birding etiquette. Because most birders are devoted to record keeping, inevitably that infamous trinity of "The Good, the Bad, and the Ugly" manifests itself in the birding culture. The Good Birder discovers, correctly identifies, and successfully brings to the attention of the rest of the birding community a super rarity (such as Red-footed Falcon in Massachusetts in 2004) so that others get to see and enjoy it. The Bad Birder correctly identifies the rarity and aggressively attempts to lay claim to its discovery even though he is *not* the birder who initially discovered it. The Ugly Birder knowingly fabricates a rarity, usually with little or no basis for its presence. For reasons no doubt linked to ego gratification, Bad and Ugly Birders occasionally try to dupe the birding community. Fortunately, the ruses of such nefarious individuals are rarely successful, and regular practitioners of these unseemly forms of birding etiquette are quickly ferreted out and ostracized.

It's not just within the birding community that questions of etiquette arise. Interacting with the nonbirding public has its challenges as well. As a youth I would conceal my binoculars whenever I found myself in the presence of nonbirders, or I would pretend to be doing something other than looking at birds (scanning for whales or taking pictures) when confronted by a curious passerby. And of course I would *never* let on that I was a birder in the company of my nonbirding contemporaries. Nowadays, I actively engage the public in discussions about birds at every opportunity, and I openly wear my binoculars in public. I daresay that it is through such practices that birding is where it is today. Don't be ashamed to be a birder — be proud, and be proactive. The birds may someday thank us!

These are just a few ways you can show consideration while birding. To see the American Birding Association's Principles of Birding Ethics, go to www.americanbirding .org/abaethics.htm.

WAYNE R. PETERSEN directs the Massachusetts Audubon Society's Important Bird Areas Program. He also leads international birding tours, lectures extensively, and has been conducting birding workshops for nearly forty years. Petersen coauthored *Birds of Massachusetts* and the *Massachusetts Breeding Bird Atlas* and contributed accounts to *The Sibley Guide to Bird Life and Behavior*.

29. *Play Fair When Sharing a Scope*
by Peter Alden

ALL BIRDERS HAVE BINOCULARS around their necks. Top birders also usually carry a spotting scope on a tripod, whose three legs stay splayed out when balanced on a shoulder. The scope's superior magnification is most useful for scanning a pond shore, mud flat, or beach.

Birding can be a competitive sport, and many people like to claim they've seen more species than other members of their circle, whether on life lists, year lists, trip lists, or locality lists. There are bragging rights if you've seen some rarity that others have missed.

On many a beginner's bird walk near home, or on a faraway birding tour, the trip leader may have the only scope, and it is important to learn how to use it and share it.

First of all, try to remember which end to look into. There's a narrow end and a large end. If you want to see what that bird would look like in the next county via an unaided eye, peer into the large end.

Most trip leaders are pretty excited about a rare find and really want you to see it. If you look in the scope and see a birdless dead branch or an empty mud flat, just say,

"Great, always wanted to see one of those." Do not disappoint your leader.

There are some simple rules to follow to ensure that a genuine rarity shows up on your list and not on everyone else's.

1. If you are taller than most of the rest of your group, be sure that the scope is elevated to its highest position comfortable for you. The others will have to balance uneasily on tiptoes or jump up and down for an erratic glimpse of the rarity.

2. Locate the focus knob with your index finger. When you've had a satisfactory view, turn it all the way clockwise or counterclockwise so that the next eager viewer will see something resembling a fog bank.

3. Take as much time as possible viewing the bird. Describe all sorts of field marks, unique behavioral quirks, and all the places you've visited and failed to see this wonderful creature. Thank the trip leader profusely. During these precious minutes, the bird will likely continue on its way before the rest of the party gets a peek.

4. Do not tell anyone if the bird does indeed fly away. That will just disappoint those who have yet to look into the scope.

5. If the bird is still there when you decide it's time to let some pushy member of your party have a chance to see

it with the scope, remember to kick one of the legs of the tripod gently. Shifting the direction of the scope just a few degrees will enable the next viewer to get a great view of some trash bird or a colorful beer can.

6. Have everyone get into a straight line directly behind you. That will ensure that they can't possibly see the bird as a speck in their binoculars. Never step sideways on leaving the scope. Step backward quickly, and you should be able to create a domino effect of falling, cursing bodies that will surely cause the rarity to wing off to an unknown destination.

7. Congratulate yourself on this great addition to your list and express your deepest heartfelt wishes that someday, somewhere, the rest of your party will get to see this rarity as well as you did on this red-letter day.

On a more serious note, a good trip leader will set the scope for the shortest member of the party and teach everyone to use it on a common bird first. Your better eye should be about one inch away (from the smaller end) and find the pale circle of light. Each person may have to adjust the focus knob a little one way or another. The leader should have the group form a line at a 90-degree angle from the direction of the scope and give each person five seconds to look. After everyone has had a chance, repeat for slightly longer views if the bird is still present. If the bird is walking or swimming, the leader should pop in and redirect the scope or lead it a little as the bird moves around. Anyone who kicks the legs of the tripod should go to the back of the line. Happy birding!

———

PETER ALDEN, of Concord, Massachusetts, has led three hundred nature and birding tours to one hundred countries for travel and museum organizations. He is principal author of the National Audubon Society's Regional Field Guide series. He organized the first-ever state-sponsored statewide biodiversity events and is president of the Nuttall Ornithological Club.

30. *Go Birding in Bad Weather*
by Bill Schmoker

M Y MOST MEMORABLE BIG Day began at midnight on May 19, 2003, under clear, starlit skies at a local marsh. Our target species were so cooperative that my Birdathon! team had a few spare minutes to enjoy the night sounds before continuing our tight itinerary to the foothills of Boulder County, Colorado, to work on owls and poorwills. It turned out that we had already experienced the high temperature for the day while enjoying the midnight marsh ambiance. A few hours later, more than one thousand feet above Boulder, the four of us watched a wet cold front roll in across the city and plains below us to the east. The city lights winked out under opaque sheets of fog and clouds, which sent calling nocturnal migrants our way for a while as they tried to skirt the bad weather. Then clouds, mist, and rain enveloped us, too, and we were in bad-weather birding mode for the rest of the day.

Not only had we seen the day's last clear skies but dry socks were becoming only a fond memory. Heavy weather delayed the morning light, inducing procrastination among the dawn chorus vocalists. Although it was tardy, peak vocalization lasted late into midmorning in the

muted light. Wearing everything we brought and struggling to keep our optics functional, we used driving intervals to revive ourselves and our equipment. By the end of the day, we had tallied 165 species in the county, besting the previous high mark by over 20 species. While Big Days are always exciting, on this day there was an extra sense of camaraderie and adventure as we dealt with weather that most folks would consider downright crummy.

People ask me, "When is the best time to go birding?" My standard answer is, "Whenever you can." Given that, there is much to be said for getting out in *bad* weather when you can. Bad weather is birdy weather: feeders get more action, migrants go to ground or water to ride out storms, and rare birds show up in unusual locations. If you wait until the storm clears, it may be too late — don't skip on a great bird just because you didn't want to get a little sleet down your collar.

Of course, bad-weather birders face perils that their fair-weather friends don't, including aching toes, numb fingers, drippy noses, frost-nipped ears, fogged or water-sheeted optics, opaque eyeglasses, and compromised cameras. Discomfort is one thing, but hypothermia can be serious. Bad-weather birding requires good layered clothing, including rain gear. Fully sealed, nitrogen-purged binoculars and scopes are musts for bad-weather birders. Of course, no matter how dry the innards of your optics are, precipitation on lens surfaces and eyeglasses will soon render them more or less useless. Be as proactive as you can about keeping your optical surfaces clear. Big-brimmed hats don't just keep the sun off your neck and face — they also keep precipitation off your optics. Hoods can be pulled forward, enveloping eyepieces within their protective enclosures. Umbrellas do the same, provided the wind is manageable. Keep a few dry, clean lens cloths squirreled away in your pockets — I cringe to see a shirttail used to wipe off expensive lenses. In a pinch, though, licking snow, rain, or even salt spray off your eyepieces can save the day.

I'm a big fan of the rubber rain guard that came with my binoculars. Besides keeping precipitation off the oculars, it also protects them from errant postnasal drip, cream cheese plops, and coffee dribbles (to mention a few contaminants my rain guard regularly intercepts). While some may consider the rain guard a hindrance, I just bring up my bins, bite the center of the guard, and pull it off as I continue to raise them to my eyes — primitive behavior, perhaps, but effective. Those who eschew the rain guard usually tuck their bins into their jackets during foul weather, holding them at the ready with hand under lapel like a posing Napoleon.

The sunshade on your spotting scope makes a good precipitation shield in inclement weather. Bad-weather birding is a time when a 45-degree angled scope may have a slight disadvantage — the upturned eyepiece uncannily seems to catch the very first speck of precipitation to fall. Use a lens cap or scope cover to protect the eyepiece when it isn't shielded by your hat brim, hood, or umbrella. I've even dropped a ball cap over my eyepiece in a sudden squall to keep it dry between viewings — an expensive hat rack indeed!

When the weather gets really rough, sometimes the best option is to use your vehicle as a portable blind, shelter, and warming hut. It's nice to have a window mount configured with the same quick release as your tripod head, so that you can pop on your spotting scope without tedious hardware adjustments. When possible, park so the wind is blowing generally from you toward the birds, giving you a dry viewing envelope in the lee of the car. When you sally out from your vehicle and later return to its warm, humid interior, you will likely get condensation on cold lens surfaces. Take advantage of your vehicle's defroster and use it like a hair dryer to get things dried off and your fingers working again.

As I write this in early March, a cold front is predicted to sweep Colorado tonight and tomorrow. Rain and snow should blast the plains, and more snow will blanket higher elevations. Tomorrow could shape up as a classic bad-weather birding day — should I look for unusual gulls at eastern reservoirs, or should I head up into the mountains for rosy-finches at feeders? Upon further thought, why not both?

A middle school science teacher, BILL SCHMOKER hails from Longmont, Colorado. He is a regional editor of *North American Birds*, vice president of the Colorado Field Ornithologists, and is associated with Leica as a digiscoping consultant. His bird photos appear in books and magazines, on Web sites, and on interpretive signage throughout North America. Bill has presented digital bird photography workshops for organizations including the American Birding Association and Western Field Ornithologists.

31. *Learn about Distribution and Weather*
by Paul Lehman

TIMING IS EVERYTHING, IN birding as well as in life. Some characteristics of avian behavior lend themselves to getting the timing just right, such as the predictable patterns of migration and distribution.

Although it is critical to learn about the field identification of birds, it is also extremely important to learn as much as you can about bird distribution, seasonal status, and habitat requirements. Understanding what is expected in a given region and at a given time of year makes a birder more aware of what would be unusual. If you believe you have found a species that is well out of range or out of season, you can make extra efforts to study it thoroughly, noting as many field marks as possible and making sure to rule out similar species.

I have seen people misidentify birds not because they didn't know the birds' field marks but because of their unfamiliarity with status and distribution. A birder may know how a Swainson's Thrush is supposed to differ from a Hermit Thrush, and both species may be regular breeders or migrants where he lives or is visiting. On the one hand, if this same person is unaware that Swainson's Thrush is almost unknown in the United States and Canada after the first few days of November, he might be tempted to report one erroneously, for example, on a Christmas Bird Count. On the other hand, if he appreciates the nuances of avian status and distribution and truly believes he has found a Swainson's in winter, then he will know at the time that the bird needs to be thoroughly documented and photographed if possible, and news of its presence quickly spread among the birding community so that others may corroborate the sighting. Yes, some birds do wander way out of their normal range and occur at unusual seasons — finding such birds is a major allure for many a birder. We need to be prepared, beforehand, for what would be unusual and treat these occurrences as such.

So how does one learn about avian status and distribution? Look at the range maps in your field guides. Buy books dealing with bird distribution: most states and provinces, and many smaller regions, have volumes dealing with just this topic. Also, read state or provincial magazines and journals that include seasonal summaries, perhaps subscribe to *North American Birds* magazine, and read as many of the regional seasonal reports as you can. Last, travel! Go birding in many regions of North America and not only in those where you can find a number of life birds. Learn the field marks of species that are potential rarities in your home region by studying good numbers of that species where it is found more commonly. There really is no better way to gain an appreciation of the status, distribution, and habitat requirements of our continent's birds.

There is a wild card, however, when it comes to birds: weather. And, okay, I admit it. I am a weather freak. Have been since I was in my teens. And I admit that my friends even accuse me of watching reruns on The Weather Channel, but understanding and closely following the weather is a crucial component of successful birding. Heading out into the field without first checking the weather forecast one or two days ahead of time, particularly during the spring and fall migration seasons, may well hinder your success.

For the birder, it is important to keep up-to-date on meteorological happenings for two reasons. First, there is the question of personal comfort and safety. For land birding, you probably will wish to avoid fifty-mile-an-hour winds; such conditions may be just the ticket, though, if you are sea-watching or chasing down the remnants of a tropical storm or hurricane, hoping to find some storm-blown avian waifs. Second is the more germane issue of the profound effects of the weather on the normal movements of birds. A successful day in the field during migration will probably depend on when and where you decide to go birding and what types of birds you are looking for — all of which are affected by the weather that day and the previous days.

It is important to remember that the weather usually does not "cause" avian migration. Migration is caused by factors such as changes in day length and variation in food supply. However, weather does affect the short-term timing, direction, and magnitude of the movement of birds. The calendar might say that it is the peak of the hawk or warbler migration, but if the weather is not conducive to such movements, there won't be very many birds to see.

Weather forecasts in the newspaper and on TV and radio are good and easily accessible. Even better is a weather radio, which continually broadcasts the official U.S. NOAA (National Oceanographic and Atmospheric Administration) and WeatherRadio Canada forecasts, severe weather alerts, tide and offshore waters information, and more. Some car models include this weather band on their factory-installed radios. Recently, a veritable flood of weather information sites have sprung up on the Internet. Some of these sites are run by for-profit businesses, and many others were established by universities. For those birders contemplating a pelagic trip, there are a numer of sites that give wind and swell information from buoys located well offshore. Information on offshore wind speed and direction or fog conditions may prove crucial to birders deciding whether or not there might be a fallout of land-bird migrants along a coastline. And there is also cable television: The Weather Channel (United States) and The Weather Network (Canada). Local forecasts, extended weekly forecasts, maps showing the positions and movements of high- and low-pressure systems from coast to coast, areas of precipitation, the upper air (jet stream) wind flow, and detailed coverage of tropical storms are all important pieces of information knowledgeable birders should use.

PAUL LEHMAN is a tour leader, author, and chief range-map specialist for the *Peterson Field Guide to Eastern Birds* and the *Peterson Field Guide to Western Birds,* the National Geographic Society, and the Sibley Field Guides. A former editor of *Birding* magazine, Lehman is also a former university instructor of geography, including meteorology.

32. *Use a Storm to Your Advantage*
by Jeffrey Bouton

WEATHER SHAPES EVERY aspect of bird migration. It dictates when and how far birds will migrate and how many species or individuals we may see. It affects our ability to view the birds and in some cases even how close flying birds will come to us. While warm, pleasant days provide a setting for enjoyable birding, crummy weather has produced some of the most memorable and spectacular birding events I've ever witnessed.

For example, drizzly days in early October reliably produce incredible air shows along the entire eastern seaboard. No advance ticketing required, just grab your waterproof binoculars and rain gear and head for the dunes. You'll find the beaches and barrier islands chock-full of Peregrine Falcons patrolling for weather-battered migrants struggling to reach land. With their blinding speed and impressive aerial maneuvers, Peregrines never fail to produce heart-pounding shows under these conditions.

"Fallouts" are another spectacle of nature that can be seen anywhere during migration. When the weather behaves just right, brightly colored warblers, tanagers, orioles, buntings, and other migrants seem to fall out of the sky en masse and brighten the landscape like living ornaments in shades of yellow, blue, red, and orange. On still nights during the peak of migration, listen for the *chip*s, *tsip*s, and *wheer*s of songbirds on the move before you retire for the evening. If you hear these calls at night and wake to a light drizzle or passing shower, this is your cue to head to your favorite local patch of birdy habitat. More often than not, the vegetation will be dripping with more than water droplets.

North winds in late April and early May have been known to cause illness among birders near the Gulf Coast of Texas. Outbreaks of this original "bird flu" are typically curable only by a visit to South Padre Island or a similar barrier island. Here these poor, sick birders endure their prescribed treatments and hope to recuperate. The prescription might read, "See hundreds of individuals of more than twenty species of warblers, and return to work tomorrow."

Another favorite weather pattern for birding is the on-shore wind. Strong winds blowing off the ocean often bring seldom-seen pelagic (oceanic) birds close to shore. This phenomenon allows the poor saps who turn green at the mere thought of stepping on a boat the opportunity to see offshore species, such as jaegers, shearwaters, and storm-petrels, from terra firma.

Of course, for the folks living hundreds of miles from

salt water, seeing one of these birds near home typically requires that mother of all onshore winds, the hurricane. After the past few years, it seems fewer birders living along the coast actually *hope* for one of these natural disasters to blow through, but I suppose if you have to endure one, you can at least hope for a good yard bird out of the deal. As one of many Floridian transplants with firsthand experience in "God's Bowling Alley," I can say there is nothing fun about being hit by one of Mother Nature's furious blows. Nonetheless, crazed storm chasers, extreme surfers, and yes, even birders are often rapt with excitement at the thought of a big storm coming ashore. Even with the sobering images of people who lost everything fresh in mind, I'd be lying if I said I hadn't appreciated the opportunity to see Sooty and Bridled Terns, storm-petrels, and other wind-swept species close to home after a big blow.

Of course, you should never intentionally put yourself in the path of a hurricane. Anyone who says "I wasn't scared" either is a liar or wasn't actually *in* the heart of a big storm. He certainly didn't experience the amazing power and noise or hear the water gurgle back up the drains as the extreme low-pressure cell roared overhead. She didn't feel her eardrums trying to abandon her head, and she wasn't huddled in her bathtub quietly praying for it to end soon. This is not where you want to be, and if you are, birding is not what you'll be thinking about.

After the storm passes, though, many birds are found deposited on large bodies of fresh water. Observers on hand shortly after the passage of a storm often report hundreds of Sooty and Bridled Terns, Brown Noddies, and even rarer species, such as Black-capped Petrels. Within twenty-four hours, however, they are typically gone. It seems that, despite the distance they've already been carried, most of these birds are well enough to return to the salt water almost immediately. So while it isn't smart to go out with downed power lines, large hanging limbs, and debris on the roads, those who do venture out immediately following a storm see a lot of unusual birds.

If you have always been a fair-weather birder, I challenge you to brave the elements once and see what you think. You don't have to cut your teeth on a hurricane, mind you, but maybe you could try heading out on a drizzly day in late April. You may see an amazing spectacle of nature unfold and learn that you, too, have a fine appreciation for birding in crummy weather.

JEFFREY BOUTON has worked as professional field ornithologist and birding tour guide for over twenty years and is now a product specialist for Leica Sport Optics. He travels the country leading field trips and giving bird-related presentations at many of the large birding festivals.

Building a Nest Egg

33. Be a Proactive Conservationist
by Paul J. Baicich

T0 HEAR SOME FOLKS talk, the use of cell phones will kill birds. (Reason: cell towers offer deadly barriers to migrating songbirds.) Using your car on a birding field trip damages the environment for birds. (Reason: your exhaust generates greenhouse gases, accelerating global warming.) Every time you turn on a light a bird dies. (Reason: coal-fired power plants produce mercury particulate, poisoning the food chain for birds.) Living in a home with glass windows kills birds. (Reason: *thump!*) Having a cat kills birds. (Reason: Tabby's a natural-born killer.) Eating seafood kills birds. (Reason: longline fisheries are killing albatross, shearwaters, and other sea birds.) Using soy products kills birds. (Reason: bird-rich old-growth prairie is giving way to soy monoculture.) Drinking supermarket blends of coffee kills birds. (Reason: the blends discriminate against bird-compatible arabica coffee.)

Now that you are fully informed — and, incidentally, completely dispirited — try to enjoy your birding!

Perhaps our messengers of avian doom should conclude: "For God's sake, stop breathing oxygen, you dolt, and save the birds!"

And perhaps not.

After all, with your demise — upon your selfless and noble refusal of oxygen — there will be plenty of *other* people out there breathing oxygen, perfectly willing to go on doing all those things that might harm Mother Earth and her birds.

Now it's time to consider a proactive bird conservation method, as opposed to one that is simply reactive. Proactive conservation can focus on a preventive approach, one that can get ahead of the curve.

Let's be clear: self-abnegation and guilt tripping over disasters around us are really not the best approaches to our bird-conservation problems. Believe me, to save birds you are *not required to slash your wrists*. There are actually modest things you can do that will help birds and their habitats.

The idea is to get ahead of the situation before it becomes an emergency of major proportions, too big for us birders to get our collective arms around. A proactive approach is an antidote to responding to perpetual crisis. To prove that contention, let me suggest just seven simple tasks:

1. CREATE A BIRD-FRIENDLY BACKYARD

You don't have to live the life of a cheerless hermit, but you *can* start at home and live by example. Favor bird-friendly native plants in your yard; host a broad selection of feeders; put up nest boxes to supplement missing cavities in dead tree branches; keep cats indoors; use glass protection to deter birds from flying into your windows.

2. DRINK SHADE-GROWN COFFEE

While you are at home, be part of the movement toward bird-compatible shade-grown coffee. The birds need it, and the coffee tastes better, too. You can also *promote this effort in your community,* encouraging others to appreciate the role that shade-grown coffee fields play in Latin America and the Caribbean. By mimicking the natural forest, these areas provide habitat for Neotropical migrant and resident birds alike. Appreciate the overlap between organic and fair-traded coffee, too.

3. BUY THE MIGRATORY BIRD STAMP

Buy the annual Migratory Bird Hunting and Conservation Stamp, commonly known as the Duck Stamp. Proceeds from its sales are used to acquire national wildlife refuge lands (fee-title and easements). It's not "just for ducks," it supports all sorts of wetland and grassland birds. Historically, waterfowl hunters have been doing all the heavy lifting in this task; it's time for birders to enlist seriously. (An additional benefit of the stamp is that it's an annual pass for refuges that charge for entry.)

4. TRANSFER EQUIPMENT

Ship field equipment to our counterparts in Latin America and the Caribbean. Birders' Exchange is the best example of this effort, but there are others, such as Optics for the Tropics. Understand that it is *not* charity but simply self-interest to link with our colleagues who are ultimately responsible with us for the joint guardianship of our migrating Neotropical birdlife.

5. SUPPORT INTERNATIONAL MIGRATORY BIRD DAY AND BIRD FESTIVALS

Support International Migratory Bird Day or a birding festival in your area. These serve to educate an increasingly curious public and to build local community support for bird-habitat conservation, especially if the events attract out-of-town birders, who will spend good money for food and lodging.

6. SUPPORT IMPORTANT BIRD AREAS

The Important Bird Areas Program (coordinated by the National Audubon Society) attempts to identify sites that are fundamental for maintaining bird populations (breeding, migration, and wintering areas). By joining to enumerate and protect these areas, you can not only identify them but also give them another dimension — serious stewardship. (Also remember that some similar programs, such as the Western Hemisphere Shorebird Reserve Network, overlap conveniently with Important Bird Areas.)

7. BE A FRIEND

Speaking of stewardship, don't neglect the opportunity to be an active "friend." Many county and local parks and, especially, national wildlife refuges have friends' groups. These are often bird-oriented; the locations involved are often Important Bird Areas; the sites all need the TLC offered by friends' groups.

Contrariwise, staying at home, windowless and in the dark, turning on the heat only when it gets bitterly cold, eating organic dandelion gruel, and recycling your nail clippings may actually add up to an infinitesimal interruption in avian slaughter. Still, you can do so many other things, and do them so much more effectively. The name of this short essay could easily have been a spinoff from this book's title: "Good Birders Don't Wear Sackcloth and Ashes."

It's not by ceasing to breathe oxygen — a metaphor, if you will — but by engaging others who breathe oxygen that we make change possible.

In the words of Roger Tory Peterson, "The truth of the matter is, the birds could very well live without us, but many — perhaps all — of us would find life incomplete, indeed almost intolerable without the birds." Birds are the portals through which so many of us understand much more of the natural world. Peterson, the master, also concluded that *knowing about birds ourselves* is one thing, but *conveying the wonder of birds and the importance of saving them to others* is quite another.

Each of us can do a little bit, making sure that the birds are protected, their habitats secure, their future in better hands. Start with these seven proactive tasks in bird conservation. In sum, they can add up to a very great deal.

Once engaged, after all, you can breathe easy. Almost.

PAUL J. BAICICH coauthored (with the late Colin Harrison) the *Princeton Field Guide to Nests, Eggs, and Nestlings of North American Birds* and has co-led a number of tours and workshops to Alaska. A member of the management board of the Prairie Pothole Joint Venture and the Waterbird Conservation Council, Baicich has recently worked for the National Wildlife Refuge Association.

34. *Make a Difference for Birds*
by Scott Weidensaul

A FEW YEARS AGO, when a crucial conservation program was in jeopardy of elimination, I posted a note on our state birding list, suggesting folks contact the governor's office to protest the plan.

They did, in droves, and the program was saved. But to my astonishment, I also heard from dozens of people who were moved in a different way — annoyed, and in some cases enraged, that I'd brought up the subject in a birding forum. "I don't subscribe to this list to read about this conservation crap," one man fumed. "I subscribe to learn where to find birds."

All I could do was wonder: where on earth does he think the birds come from? Maybe some aging factory in a gray industrial town, where a greasy machine chugs all day long, spitting out species after species onto an assembly line? *Clunk,* a Song Sparrow. *Whir,* an Eared Grebe. *Thunk,* a Costa's Hummingbird. Box 'em up and ship 'em out, boys!

Birds come from bird habitat — and we have a good deal less of it every day. The pressures on birds grow ever more intense as the human population of the United States passes the 300 million mark. Some places, such as my home state of Pennsylvania, have lost more forest and field habitat to development in the past twenty-five years than in all of the preceding two hundred. As the land goes, so go the birds on which our hobby depends.

So watching birds means protecting them, too, and the places on which they depend — or at least, it ought to. *Actively* protecting them, not just with kind thoughts and good wishes but with your time, your vote, and your money. If you're a birder, you need to be an active conservationist, too.

It doesn't have to involve a lot of time, or a lot of money. But it should involve a lot of your passion. You don't have to be a protest-march conservationist, the kind who lies down in front of a bulldozer. But you should be a letter-to-the-editor-writing conservationist, a congressperson-calling conservationist; someone who keeps up on the issues and puts his efforts where his binoculars are. The kind who joins not just the local bird club but also the local friends of the sanctuary group, someone who supports the regional conservancy that's protecting open spaces, who calls local politicians to account when they make decisions that will have negative impacts on wildlife and wildlife habitat.

And because birds are not a partisan issue, it's easy to be a voting conservationist, the sort who takes birds into account when casting a ballot, whether it's for president or for the township board of supervisors.

We are told there are now tens of millions of birders in the United States. That ought to make us a pretty formidable bloc — and we would be, if we all voted consistently on behalf of the birds. If we did that — and let our representatives know *why* we voted that way — you'd see a scramble to make bird conservation a priority across party lines and at all levels of government.

Birders need to take a page from hunters and anglers, who have been told for nearly a century, by the elders of their sports, that they have a responsibility to be agents of conservation. As a hunter and fisherman myself, I'm proud of the contributions we've made, largely through license fees and federal excise taxes on equipment and ammunition, which pump hundreds of millions of dollars into conservation programs every year. The federal Duck Stamp, which every waterfowl hunter is required to buy, has since the 1930s paid for much of the national wildlife refuge system.

Birders, who have long enjoyed a hobby that is only as expensive as we choose to make it, need to embrace the same ethic. We should lobby for long-stalled, dedicated excise taxes on birdseed and binoculars and other birding gear, not because we like spending more money but because it's the right thing to do — because that money will breathe new life into conservation programs and land protection to benefit nongame birds. With our rapidly

growing numbers, birders could have a far greater benefi-
cial impact on wildlife conservation than consumptive
users, such as hunters, could ever hope to achieve.

In the meantime, buy a federal Duck Stamp even if you
don't hunt; your local post office sells them, and it's the best
fifteen bucks you can spend for wildlife. (It'll also get you
in free to any refuge that charges an admission fee, which
is a nice bonus.) If your state sells waterfowl or nongame
stamps, buy them annually as well.

There are simple things you can do day in and day out
to help birds, from planting berry-rich shrubs in your
yard to drinking bird-friendly coffee. (See page 161 for
more ideas.) And if you really want to make a difference,
my friend Kenn Kaufman has suggested that you not
count a new species on your life list until you have also
done something concrete to help that species. Extreme?
Maybe — but think of the momentum for change such an
attitude would create.

Look, I know you're not one of those callous, greedy
types who view birds only as some kind of feathered inven-
tory, one to which you have a perfect right but no responsibility. Few birders are. The rest of us just need to be engaged, to become the kinds of birders who give back to the
creatures on which our obsession depends — and whose
continued survival is now in our hands.

It just takes a little effort, and a rededication to the birds. Isn't a Townsend's Warbler, singing from the bough of a Doug fir, worth it? A Swainson's Hawk soaring beneath a perfect Plains sky, a Hermit Thrush filling the North Woods with song, or a shearwater slicing through the cold sea wind?

Of course.

SCOTT WEIDENSAUL is the author of more than two dozen books on nature and wildlife, including the Pulitzer Prize–nominated *Living on the Wind* and his most recent book, *Return to Wild America*. He lives in the mountains of eastern Pennsylvania.

35. *Write It Down: Making a Calendar*

by Julie Zickefoose

IT WAS ONE OF THOSE things that local naturalists get asked to do, and it seemed like it would be worth trying. The Marietta Natural History Society needed a calendar for its monthly newsletter, something that would help its readers track the seasons.

As a compulsive recorder of all things interesting, I had the information, in spiral-bound books and later in computer files. All that remained to do was to comb through it, looking for bird events worthy of inclusion on this calendar.

I made a generic calendar page for each month and started sifting through my notes. The most helpful ones were in two dog-eared copies of *The Birdwatcher's Three-Year Notebook,* a spiral-bound blank calendar that had space for three years' worth of entries on each page. Eureka! Six years' worth of data. Though my winter notes were a bit sparse, as spring crept on, my writing became smaller and smaller. By April my notes were running up the sides of the pages and into the margins. It was a graphic illustration of how much happens in a short time as spring rushes in.

Quickly, it became apparent that I couldn't limit this

calendar to the requested bird events. There were wild-flowers and frogs, snakes and butterflies vying for attention, too. Each had its own arrival date or, more properly, the date I first noticed it in a given year. I came up with average arrival dates for many species and inked them in on my rapidly filling pages.

There was a fairly narrow range of dates for each one, and some were satisfyingly precise; woodcocks almost always begin their nuptial flights on February 19 in Whipple. Fox Sparrows and Killdeer come in a few days later. Great Blue Herons row over, croaking, and before you know it, it's March and spring starts to rev up. Spring peepers make the swales sing around the sixth of March. The sweet, bouncing-ball song of the first Field Sparrow transforms our meadow around the twelfth. Skunk scent wafts across the miles at night as these nocturnal animals emerge from hibernation and look for mates. Chipping Sparrows make sure to arrive before spring's first official day. And when the Brown Thrasher begins to sing, on March 28, I'd better have my peas planted.

Every year, I try to determine the date when the Dark-eyed Juncos leave for the boreal nesting grounds. This is harder to do than it would seem, because these ubiquitous winter visitors' spring trills are so similar to those of Chipping Sparrows that one seems to segue into the next. The juncos slip away quietly, and one day (around April 18, as it happens), it occurs to me that they are gone. This usually dawns on me as I'm hanging up feeders for the first Ruby-throated Hummingbirds, who arrive on the seventeenth. Pandemonium breaks loose around April 20 every year, when Black-and-white, Hooded, Black-throated Green, and Nashville Warblers arrive at once. A day later, the Whip-poor-wills strike fear into the hearts of moths everywhere with their vehement songs. At this point I am practically drunk on springtime, and it's all I can do to drag myself out of the gardens in time for bed; I'd rather stay out, grubbing in the earth, listening to the woodcocks and Whip-poor-wills.

May, of course, is a blur, ushered in by Indigo Buntings, who appear on the first, feasting on dandelion seeds in the spring rain. Later migrants flood in on the third: Magnolia Warblers, Common Yellowthroats, Chestnut-sided Warblers. Rose-breasted Grosbeaks appear, like gaudy ornaments hung on our feeders. How I wish they could stay. By May 6, all my bluebird boxes are full of sky blue eggs; some are even breaking to reveal coral pink squirmers. The first Field Sparrows are already fledging by May 18, even as the boreal flycatchers are still migrating through; we listen for the husky *Way-beer!* of the Alder; the *hic-three-beers!* of the Olive-sided. The first lightning bugs always take us by surprise on May 22; nothing is more evocative of summer than their lazy blinks over a twilight meadow.

And so the year goes. Each month has its arrivals and departures; August's bird movements are my favorites of all, for it's then that I see the crazily plumaged young of the year and say goodbye to our summer breeders for another winter. Great drifts of Common Nighthawks row over on the twenty-second; we'd miss them completely unless we knew to crane our necks skyward. What a thing to miss. The calendar tells us when to look.

Writing all this down was more than an exercise; it was a chance to savor the progress of the year. And it was an affirmation that there is a time and a season for everything. Witnessing this is one thing; writing it down and recording it for posterity is quite another. For me, it is the only way truly to understand the passing of the seasons. My calendar, twelve photocopied pages in a paper clip, is now one of my most treasured possessions. I reach for it whenever a bird arrives, and it's now marked up with colored annotations of early and late arrival dates.

All naturalists are looking for keys to the cosmos, for ways of connecting with and understanding this great wheel of events turning around us all the time. Scientists studying global warming in Great Britain are turning to the journals of amateur naturalists and bird watchers there. Their careful notes have helped to document an average shift of fifteen days toward the early side in the breeding cycles of many birds, and the blooming times of certain plants, over the last fifty years. But all animals and plants don't respond equally; some haven't begun reproducing earlier. This shift could put some species in grave danger. If a plant blooms before its pollinators emerge, it may never set seed. If a bird breeds before caterpillar outbreaks occur, nestlings may starve. The English Sparrow and European Starling are both on precipitous declines in Great Britain. The journals of naturalists like you and me may hold the keys to help us understand these phenomena.

The difference between someone who enjoys nature and someone who is called an expert may be a simple spiral-bound notebook. Take notes. Make a calendar. You'll love what happens. As Roger Tory Peterson often said, "If you don't write it down, it never happened."

———

JULIE ZICKEFOOSE is the author of *Letters from Eden,* a book of paintings and essays. She began her career as a field biologist for The Nature Conservancy, became a magazine and book illustrator, then moved to illustrating her own stories, gleaned from experiences with wild birds and animals. Her monthly commentaries bring glimpses of Appalachia to NPR's *All Things Considered. Bird Watcher's Digest* has published more than forty of her articles and seventeen cover paintings by her since 1986.

36. *Learn from Your Mistakes: How Not to Hide from Birds*

by Tim Gallagher

ONE OF THE PRIMARY skills of a bird photographer is the ability to sit quietly and motionlessly for sometimes hours on end in uncomfortable positions to get a great shot. I guess I have a somewhat stoical bent, which is probably why I took up wildlife photography. I've always prided myself on being able to stand a lot of physical discomfort. Whenever I built a bird blind, I never gave any thought to how long I'd be spending inside or how I could make it a little more comfortable. Well, I've changed. Perhaps I'm a little wiser — or maybe just older — but comfort now looms very large when I'm designing a blind. I had to learn the hard way how *not* to hide from birds.

One important lesson I've learned is never to build a blind that is too small or too low to be reasonably comfortable. Once, many years ago, I set up a blind measuring three feet wide by six feet long by eight inches high — not as large as a comfortable casket. I was photographing some nesting avocets, and I wanted my pictures to show the world from their perspective, eye to eye, right at ground level. I figured I could put my camera and telephoto lens on a beanbag and lie flat on the ground, getting shots of the birds striding past, foraging, or sitting on their nest. It was a great idea, in theory, and I did get a few photographs that I still like. But eight inches of vertical space is agonizingly low. I had to stay flattened out completely. I could barely breathe, and I couldn't even roll onto my side to change positions. Moreover, the sand beneath me was far wetter than I had anticipated. Before long, my stomach was drenched, while my back was scorching in the prairie sun. It was impossible to change film, and the heat, the fishy stench of the sand, the sand flies in my face . . . Well, it was not fun.

This could all have been avoided if I had just set up a three-foot-high blind. Then I could have changed positions whenever I became stiff. I also could have set up two cameras — one at ground level, another a couple of feet higher on a tripod — and shot from different angles, varying my body position as well as my photographs. I should have put down a ground cloth to keep my equipment (and me) away from the moisture and bird guano. And I should have brought some water, a little food, and maybe a small towel to wipe the sweat from my face.

Another lesson I learned the hard way was to choose very carefully the material I use to construct blinds. One of the stupidest things I've done trying to hide from birds —

and there have been many — occurred one summer about fifteen years ago, when I was traveling through Manitoba with my friend Lang Elliott, a nature-sound recordist and author. We had found a small island on a prairie lake that had nesting colonies of White Pelicans and Double-crested Cormorants, and I was eager to photograph them. The only problem was that I hadn't brought a blind with me. I stopped at a local hardware store to buy camouflage material, and all they had was a huge, thick plastic tarp with a brown-and-green leaf pattern printed on it. I figured I could cut it up into smaller sheets for the sides and top and then staple it to a frame made of two-by-four pine studs.

I decided to start with the cormorants. Although they're common, I wanted to get some shots of the grotesque, prehistoric-looking young birds, reaching out toward their parents with their snakelike black necks. Lang ferried me to the island and stayed there while I pounded the two-by-fours into the ground and attached the pieces of tarp with a staple gun. The idea was that he would wait until I had built the blind and sealed myself up inside, then paddle away, so the birds would think we had both gone. He said he would come back in two or three hours to check on me.

Talk about the greenhouse effect. The tarp was made of waterproof plastic, so it didn't breathe at all. As the sun rose higher, the blind became hotter and steamier inside, and the eyepiece on my camera fogged up. At first I thought it was funny. There I was, gagging on the stench of rotting fish, and I couldn't even take any pictures. Then it got scary. After an hour, the blind was as hot as an oven. Sweat flowed profusely from every pore in my body, and the steaming air, rich with carbon dioxide, was barely breathable. Another half-hour and I was getting delirious and disoriented. But if I stepped outside the blind, the birds would have been frightened away from their nests and may have had to stay away for a long time while I waited for Lang.

I finally dug out my Swiss Army knife and cut a small slit in the back of the blind, away from the birds, so I could suck in some fresh air. It wasn't enough. I enlarged the slit and pushed my entire head outside. I was still gasping for air like a spent salmon an hour later, when Lang came back.

Okay, I almost died out there on that stinking island in Manitoba, but at least I've never used the wrong material on a blind again. In a different situation — perhaps in rain or snow — the plastic tarp might have been fine, but on that blazing hot island, I should have used a breathable material, such as burlap or cotton. I wish I could say I've learned every possible lesson and will always do things the smart way from now on. Unfortunately, that's not how my life tends to go. There are still plenty of mistakes to be made, and I'm sure I'll make a lot of them in the years ahead.

TIM GALLAGHER is an award-winning author, editor, and wildlife photographer. A lifelong birder, he is currently editor in chief of *Living Bird* magazine, published by the Cornell Lab of Ornithology. His most recent book is *The Grail Bird: The Rediscovery of the Ivory-billed Woodpecker*.

37. *Go Digital for Bird Photography*
by Arthur Morris

B ACK IN THE OLD days — that is, before the great popularity of digital photography — very few birders were seen afield with an intermediate telephoto lens. Don't get me wrong, there have been increasing numbers of serious bird photographers out there over the past two decades with big telephoto lenses, but I am referring to folks who are birders first and foremost but like to have a lens over the shoulder when they head out for a day's birding.

The increased effective focal lengths (and the resulting increases in magnification) that come hand in hand with most digital cameras have enabled more hard-core birders to get into bird photography. But the advantages of digital don't end with more focal length bang for your buck. Film speed, or ISO, determines the sensitivity of the film or imaging sensor to light. The higher the ISO, the faster the shutter speed you can use. Fast shutter speeds allow you to make sharp images, especially when handholding intermediate telephoto lenses. The problem with film is that, once you put a roll of film into the camera, you are stuck

with that film speed. If the light levels drop, you simply will not be able to create sharp images. With digital, you can change the ISO setting as needed. If light levels drop, simply set a faster ISO. Additionally, with film, the quality at ISO 400 is marginal at best; it is very poor at ISO 800. With good digital cameras, image quality at ISO 400 is superb, and at ISO 800, it can be excellent (except in images with large dark areas). And if I need the speed, I do not hesitate to use ISO 1600 or even ISO 3200. In these instances, digital noise (equivalent to the graininess evident in film) may be noticeable, but there are several fairly easy ways to reduce the visible effects of noise.

Another advantage of digital for the recreational photographer is that all quality digital cameras offer a histogram that can be viewed with each image. A histogram is a graph representing the various tonalities in an image. With just a bit of study, it is easy to interpret each histogram and then adjust the exposure if need be. Digital photographers can make a single image of a given subject, check the histogram, set the correct exposure compensation, and be assured that each subsequent exposure will be perfect (as long as the light remains constant). With film, determining the best exposure was a challenge even for folks with decades of experience.

Here are some tips for digital photographers who are birders at heart.

1. Purchase quality used equipment and you can get started in digital with an investment of two thousand dollars or even a bit less.
2. Take the time to learn to evaluate a histogram and make the exposure changes needed to ensure a perfect exposure every time.
3. Always bring your equipment with you when you are birding. You can bet that the one day you decide not to, some gorgeous bird will just sit right in front of you. In threatening or drizzly weather, use a plastic trash bag to protect your equipment.
4. During migration, or when working with inordinately tame birds, be sure to have an extension tube in your pocket. Using one allows you to focus closer than the minimum focusing distance of your lens. When waves of migrants pass by, you may encounter some passerines sitting in one spot, too tired to move. Often, you will be able to walk right up to such individuals. Having an extension tube will allow you to make the most of these lucky days.

If you are a hard-core birder just getting started in digital bird photography, be careful out there. You just might become a passionate bird photographer and wind up trading your Leica 10 × 40s and your Kowa scope for a big lens.

ARTHUR MORRIS is widely recognized as North America's premier bird photographer. His images and articles are published regularly in books, magazines, and calendars around the world. His how-to book, *The Art of Bird Photography,* is the classic work on the subject, and the follow-up, *The Art of Bird Photography II,* has just been released on CD only. Morris is a columnist for *Popular Photography* and has been a Canon contract photographer since 1995, having been selected as one of the original group of fifty-five in Canon's Explorers of Light program. Learn more about Morris and Birds as Art at www.birdsasart.com.

38. *Dump the Gear*

by Richard Crossley

I AM OFTEN ASKED, "What are you — photographer or birder?" Considering that for years I have told people it is impossible to be both, I am now in a pickle. I started birding at age ten; by the time I was fourteen it was starting to take over my life; by nineteen it *was* my life; and at twenty-one I had put myself in numerous situations in which it could have taken my life. I dragged my wife across the Atlantic Ocean so I could live with the birds in Cape May. So I am a confirmed birder.

Although I have played with photography for twenty years, it wasn't until the early days of coauthoring *The Shorebird Guide* that my life would take another obsessive turn. When told by respected professional bird photographers that it was impossible to get the photographs we needed for the book, we could respond in only one way: prove them wrong. (Although when I think of the many family dinners I missed just to get a flight photo of one bird, an American Woodcock, I realize that perhaps it is I who was wrong.)

Now, four years on, I go nowhere without a camera. I hate to say this, but I occasionally get way into the field before realizing I forgot my binoculars. I suppose if I can't be both a photographer and a birder, that makes me a bird photographer with a bit of inside scoop on birds. And yes, they are tricky little so-and-sos. They move fast and are almost never as close as we want them to be. So if you do what bird photographers are supposed to do — put a big camera lens with lots of cords, flashes, and other rigamarole on a big tripod and walk up close to birds while they smile at you — well, good luck.

Birds are scared by the same actions as we are, and they react just as we would to an elephant. Change is scariest. If a group of people stand quietly but then someone makes a quick movement or speaks loudly, the sudden change will surely make the birds fly away. Constant loud noise is often not a problem if there are no sudden changes in the volume: clicking your camera as you get closer to a bird makes the bird familiar with the sound.

Back to the elephant. If it were on its knees or lying down, would it be less threatening? Absolutely. Okay, so you know what is coming next. That's right, down you get. In the right environment, such as on the beach or in short grass, crawling is the way to go.

But what about all my gear? Now I am going to get into really sticky ground with a lot of photographers, but I say dump it! Let's have a look at why. Tripod: what do you need it for? Rest your lens on the ground, your hand, or your binoculars, depending on what angle you need. It is amazing how many natural tripods, such as trees and fences, there really are. Personally, I prefer to be without a tripod, because it limits movement and makes it very difficult to shoot moving birds. If I intend to be relatively stationary, then I will use one. If you are able to handhold your lens, though, you can cover much larger areas in search of your prey. Then, when you see your target, you can take shots immediately. Handholding also makes it easier to get closer to the subject. The downside is not being able to shoot at very slow shutter speeds. But at high f-stops, I get the depth of field and the scenic backgrounds I love. If you shoot "wide open" (low f-stops), taking sharp photos should be no problem, particularly with an image-stabilized lens and a digital camera that shoots good images at high ISOs.

What about other equipment, such as flashes; are they vital? In poor light they make the image more visually appealing. However, they do not create an accurate portrayal of the image as we see it. As someone who has spent many years studying the minutiae of bird identification and the effect light has, I find the use of flash particularly distracting. I've also been influenced by a two-year stint in Japan, where bird photographers place much more emphasis on natural light, and images tell the story about the bird and where it lives.

Here in the United States, the image of choice seems to be a close-up with sharp feather detail (probably with a bit of fill flash) and a nice unicolored background — an image we essentially never see in reality through binoculars or with the naked eye. But it sells! It is not my cup of tea, so I admit to a bit of bias when I say life goes on without a flash.

So what is a good image? My dad, an impressionistic artist in the van Gogh mold, describes art as "a pleasing arrangement of color and shapes." When I think about it, this is how I see birds. I see shape and movement in both black-and-white and color in the beautiful places where they live. I do not see them in incredible detail, close up with a unicolored backdrop — do you? And the answer to the question "What is a good image?" is easy — one that looks good to you!

———

RICHARD CROSSLEY was born in England. He has lived in Europe, Asia, and North America, and is an expert on the birds of all three regions. He is a master at identifying birds at a distance based on size and structure. Crossley's unique perspective on photography, birds, and color can be seen in *The Shorebird Guide*.

39. *Learn by Drawing*
by David Sibley

For me, drawing birds has always been a part of watching them. Drawing is a way of mentally "capturing" the bird and is really a form of interaction. While it might be easier and in some ways better to point a camera at a bird and simply *take* its picture, making a drawing requires you to slow down and engage in a sort of visual dialogue with the bird. "The head is rounded . . . like this? Maybe more like this. Yes, but then the bill isn't quite right. *Oh,* yes, I see, the head is held a little higher."

I always carry paper with me so that I can sketch or take notes — a full-size pad when I can or just a pocket notebook — and I look for things that are noteworthy: an observation about bill shape, the posture of a singing bird, a tail pattern. I think drawing is the single best thing any birder can do to learn more about birds.

I saw my first White-winged Crossbill when I was twelve, and I could have identified it and added it to my life list simply by noticing the white wing bars and the crossed bill, but I wanted to draw it as a kind of souvenir. And that meant that I had to pay attention to the head

shape, the exact shape and position of the white markings on the wings, the color of the undertail coverts, and on and on. My finished drawings were not particularly good or useful by themselves, but my head was filled with the colors and shapes and movements of the White-winged Crossbill.

The process of drawing begins with seeing the whole bird and then forces you to simplify that image and find the essential lines to represent the bird on paper. Drawing birds (or trees, or houses, or whatever) is a great way to learn the fundamental characteristics that distinguish one from another, as well as the things that are shared.

The next time you find some cooperative birds, try some sketches. Just take a few minutes to give the birds your complete attention. You'll be surprised at what you learn. As you interview the bird about its head shape, you might notice the way it hops or how it searches for food. Try this process once a week, and you'll find that you look at birds in a different way. You'll look at a blackbird and a goldfinch and actually notice that the shapes and postures of their heads are different.

You can toss the sketches in a drawer or in the trash. They are not as important as the process. The souvenir you are collecting is the familiarity and the understanding that comes from the act of drawing.

DAVID SIBLEY is the author and illustrator of a series of highly acclaimed books about birds and birding. He is the recipient of the Roger Tory Peterson Award, presented by the American Birding Association for a lifetime of achievement. Sibley lives in Concord, Massachusetts, with his wife and two sons.

40. *Practice Seeing*
by Chuck Hagner

LAST SUMMER A ROGUE Wisconsin storm knocked a robin's nest out of the silver maple in my backyard and littered the ground below with twigs. But the feeders didn't fall; they just swung wildly on their hooks. By the time the wind had died down and rays of afternoon sun were shooting through the remaining storm clouds, a handful of finches had materialized, seemingly out of thin air, and were eyeing the feeders. In an instant, and long before my dog sniffed out the nest among the fallen branches, they were busy snatching seeds out of the tubes while hanging upside down from their tiny plastic perches.

Whether they were the same sunshine yellow birds with black foreheads and wings and dark, shiny eyes that I had watched at my feeders the day before, I couldn't say. What effect the storm had on their sudden appearance was an open question as well. What I knew for sure was what I could see, and what I could see richly repaid me for the effort I invested in observing: the goldfinches were using only one foot to hold on to their perches, not two.

I realize that it's quite a ways from a pair of tube feeders hanging from the branches of the tree in my Wisconsin backyard to a painting hanging in the Kunstmuseum in Basel, Switzerland.

My backyard is on the north side of Milwaukee, and the tree, now taller than my house, stands directly outside our kitchen window. Its leaves turn a dazzling yellow each autumn; the feeders are popular with goldfinches year-round.

Basel and its museum are just a short train ride from Freiburg im Breisgau, a university town in southwestern Germany where I studied as an undergraduate. To be sure, most of my study time back then was occupied with the literature of the Weimar Republic, not with art (and not with finches, either), but my favorite class was on the Renaissance of the Upper Rhine. It was the reason for my first trip to the Kunstmuseum.

The professor who taught the class assigned each of his students a work of art that was on public view either in or around Freiburg. Then he told us to study it, in person if possible, and write a description of it.

The assignment sounded simple and, since travel was involved, fun, but there was a catch: when we wrote our descriptions, we were forbidden to interpret what we saw. That is, we weren't allowed to name movements, styles, or schools or to try to place the paintings in cultural or historical contexts. We couldn't repeat significant events from the artists' lives or relate stories about the people and places shown in the works. We were forbidden to explain the

meaning of symbols, or even to suggest that objects repre-
sented in the paintings were symbols.

Nein danke, said our professor. And he meant it. He
would mark down our papers for every instance of inter-
pretation we included. We couldn't even name names unless they appeared in the artist's hand. To get a good grade,
we simply had to put into words what we saw and nothing
more — we had to do the same type of careful observation
work that good bird watchers always do and leave the
naming, conclusion drawing, and interpreting for later.

I remember reminding myself to look hard as I stood
gazing at the work of art that had been assigned to me: *The
Body of the Dead Christ in the Tomb,* an oil painting on
wood by Hans Holbein the Younger. The piece is extraordinary, even grisly, and sure to evoke a response in any
viewer, especially in viewers who know the story of the
Crucifixion and Easter, as I do. Viewing it, I felt the seductive tug of recalled oratorios, catechism lessons, and artwork, and I gave in to the urge to start piecing together the
story of the Passion, to walk a mental Via Dolorosa. I
began considering the Resurrection as well, but then I
caught myself.

My assignment was to describe the painting, not interpret it. And because of that assignment, I can say that I
truly saw it. Even today I can close my eyes and see a rec-
tangular work more than seventy inches long and only a

foot tall, depicting the interior of a shallow stone crypt, viewed from the side. In it lies the body of a tall, skinny, bearded man, naked but for a white cloth draped over the hips. His head rests at the left end of the painting, his feet to the right. The man's legs are unbent; his right arm lies along his side. His mouth and eyes stand open. His skin is sallow. The upper surface of the one visible hand is unnaturally blackened, as is the top of the right foot. The skin covering his ribs has been pierced.

Writing such as this will sound familiar to any birders who have shouldered the burden of reporting a bird spotted at a time of year or in a corner of the world where it has never shown up previously or normally doesn't occur. Unlucky souls; if they lacked a photograph or video image of the rarity, other bird watchers would have to decide whether to accept or reject the sightings based solely upon how well the discoverers described what they saw. But as I learned in Basel, finding words isn't difficult. It's the seeing that you have to practice — seeing without preconceptions.

CHUCK HAGNER is the editor in chief of *Birder's World* magazine as well as a book editor and nature writer. He is the author of *Wings of Spring: Courtship, Nesting, and Fledging* and the field guide *Guide to Ducks and Geese*.

41. *Don't Forget the Peripherals*
by Robert A. Braunfield

IT OCCURRED TO ME while writing an essay entitled "Birdwatching Is about Watching Birds" that not only do I enjoy watching birds but I enjoy all the little things that come along with being out watching birds. Now, you may think I'm speaking of botanizing, insect identifying, or amateur geology. I'm really referring to those little extras that, whether through one's own doing or quite serendipitously, can make a day out in the field much more meaningful.

Here, then, is a short list of just a few of those things I call "peripherals":

- Plan your birding route around a great diner. That's right. If it's out of the way, all the better. You never know what you'll find when you go down that road you've never taken before. (I found a pond full of avocets by going out of my way once.) And what could be better than starting your day sitting groggy-eyed at a counter with a piece of homemade pie and a cup of coffee poured by a waitress who calls you "hon"?
- Don't have a great diner nearby? Okay, take some food. A most memorable experience for me was searching

for Bald Eagle nests in the northern part of Connecticut years ago. It was a typical New England winter's day when we transferred to our friend's Jeep for the under-heated and overjostled trip into a reservoir area. We turned from the main road onto a series of rocky dirt roads, whose distance and state of disrepair made the trip seem even colder and more jostling than it probably really was. When at last we reached our destination deep in the middle of the forest by the lake's edge, our driver stepped out of the vehicle, lifted the hood, and produced hot pastrami sandwiches, perched upon the engine manifold, where they'd been heating perfectly the whole way. A most memorable day indeed. I don't recall if we found any eagle nests. Let's see . . . No, none at all. But those sandwiches . . .

- So, what about a beer at the end of a hot, late spring day, as you sit on the hood of your car watching night herons fly by on their way to work the late shift? A friend and I would meet occasionally on a hilltop over-looking the river — he'd bring the thermos of beer, and I'd bring the container of olives. A Great Horned Owl would appear on its snag on cue, perfectly silhou-etted against the setting sun as the Whip-poor-wills started in. Don't drink? Bring a thermos of tea. You get the idea.

- Share birds with others. Show birds to people around you. Not in a crazy Jane Hathaway way, of course. Try to act normal. Try, if you can, to point out birds with normal-sounding names, not things with the word *breast* or *semi-palmated* in their names. It once took me quite a while to convince a Central Park police officer to let me go after I attempted to point out a sapsucker to two female joggers I had thought seemed interested.

  And what's more fun than showing birds to little kids? Let me rephrase that. What's more fun than showing birds to a little kid who's quiet in the woods and is pretty interested in learning about birds? Don't have one like that? Borrow one. I borrowed one who, at the age of six, could get her new binoculars on a Chipping Sparrow far up on a roof and exclaim, "Look at the red cap!"

- Check out the used book store along the way. Of course, you read your field guides, probably even some bird publications and journals. But check out the old writers, such as Neltje Blanchan, Mabel Osgood Wright, even Arthur Allen and George Sutton. And don't forget the poets. Has anyone evoked bird imagery like Emily Dickinson?

- Stop at that yard sale on the way home! Why drive by? Where do you think I got half my tools, a third of my books, and most of the indispensable stuff on my studio walls? An original Audubon elephant folio print? No, not yet. But I know someone who did. A first-edition Peterson *Field Guide to the Birds*? Yes, I did. A trunk full of *Nature* magazines from the 1920s? Yes, and I use them often, too. A boxload of old Super 8 home movies of some unknown family's trips out West in the 1960s, with lots of birds peppered throughout the scenery? Okay, I admit it, I did buy it. And there were even some silent westerns thrown in for good measure.

Now I'm really looking forward to the upcoming migration season, so while I'm out contemplating those warblers' lives and ways, I can also be looking for that Super 8 projector along the way.

ROBERT A. BRAUNFIELD is an artist and naturalist living in Hadlyme, Connecticut. His work includes paintings, cartoons, sculptures, and writings about birds. If forced to make a decision on his favorite bird, he would choose the catbird.

42. *If You're Sure of Yourself, Stand Your Ground: Between a Rock and an Owl*

by John Kricher

M Y ADVICE TO NEW birders is to believe what you see, but only after you've thought about it. Case in point: my first sighting of a male Summer Tanager was on a May morning during the peak of spring migration, the bird foraging among newly opened oak leaves in my backyard in suburban Philadelphia. Alas, it should have been a Scarlet Tanager, because Summer Tanagers were then, nearly a half century ago, really rare around the City of Brotherly Love. And, to complicate matters, I was new to birding and had not yet seen any species of tanager. My mentors each told me, "You saw a Scarlet, not a Summer. Summers aren't around here." But why didn't it have black wings, I kept asking myself. Did I somehow miss them? Why did it look so much like Peterson's rendering of a Summer Tanager? I almost caved and changed the check mark in my Peterson guide, but a couple of weeks later, at Hawk Mountain, I saw a male Scarlet. There could be no confusing the two species. *Scarlet* really meant scarlet! Peterson got it right in his field guide. I realized I

had, indeed, been fortunate enough to have seen a Summer, well out of range perhaps, but a Summer Tanager nonetheless.

Look carefully, study the bird carefully, and think carefully about what you see; then believe what you see even when counseled to the contrary.

Nearly four decades ago, not too long after moving to Massachusetts, I went to one of my favorite birding spots, Plum Island. There I was in the land of the legendary Ludlow Griscom, a man renowned for his identification skills. I was birding in the state that Roger Tory Peterson had written about in almost reverential tones, for the sheer numbers of birders as well as their considerable field skills. It doesn't get any better than Massachusetts, or so I thought.

It was a cold and blustery winter day, the kind of day when birding from the car seems far preferable to any alternative, other than staying home and watching a football game on TV. I was slowly driving along the marsh when I saw the distinctive shape of a big white owl. I had hoped to see a Snowy Owl that day and felt pretty sure I would. Other trips to Plum Island and nearby Salisbury Beach in winter usually produced a Snowy Owl or two. And there it was, in the distance. Who could mistake that distinctive hulking, oval shape? I would get a decent look if I set up my spotting scope. So I braved the wind chill, got out of the car, and soon was studying the bird. The shape was right, but something bothered me. I kept futzing with the focus on my old scope but could not resolve the image very clearly. It was a bright day, and there was too much haze. The bird was, after all, distant. Oh well, maybe it would fly closer. I waited, and it didn't. I was still bothered. There was something . . .

A caravan of automobiles approached. Soon I was surrounded by twenty birders with binoculars and scopes. They quickly and efficiently set up their optics and set to looking out at the owl. These were the Massachusetts birders I had heard about — organized, armed with optics, confident. One individual, obviously the field trip leader, looked at me as he asked, "You on the Snowy?" I said I had been looking at it, and he mumbled something about it "having been around all week." I mentioned that I could not make out its face very clearly, and he replied, "Haze." He made some remarks to the group, and then he offered me a look in his scope. I still couldn't make out its face and said so. I blurted, "Are you sure it's a bird?" His reply was curt. "It's a Snowy Owl. You can wait around if you want, but we have other birds to see. There's a drake Barrow's near the Chain Bridge. Good luck." The caravan moved on.

I went to lunch. The burger was delightfully greasy, and it was wonderful to be in out of the cold. I began working on my checklist but balked at the tick for Snowy Owl.

I didn't feel right about checking it. And then it hit me. The wind. The owl was not facing into the wind. Its head was facing away from the wind. But the wind was strong, and the feathers on the bird's back and head should have been blowing. I never saw any feathers blowing the entire time I observed it. The Snowy Owls I had seen in previous visits all had some degree of blowing feathers. What made this one different?

I went back. Sure enough, though it had been a full hour since I had seen it, there it was, positioned the same. Not a feather was ruffling. I had to know.

Hiking out over a frozen marsh riddled with channels is not easy work, but I angled around, hopped a channel or two, and eventually got much closer. I kept my eyes on the owl as I made my way toward it. It seemed quite oblivious of me. I got so close that I didn't even need the scope I had dutifully carried with me. Binoculars were sufficient to reveal that the thing was a rock, a boulder, didn't even look like an owl from this vantage point. So that was why it had no face and its feathers were unruffled in the stiff winter wind. A snowy rock! Haze! Yeah, right.

I could provide the date of this little cautionary tale but won't. Perhaps you were out there that day among the hordes of birders, and maybe it was even your life Snowy Owl. You might have been with the car caravan that stopped and checked it off. I hope that in all the intervening years you've seen many Snowies. But if by some chance you were there at Plum Island that day, you didn't.

JOHN KRICHER is a professor of biology at Wheaton College, Norton, Massachusetts. His books include *Galapagos: A Natural History, A Neotropical Companion,* and three ecology field guides *(Eastern Forests, Rocky Mountain and Southwestern Forests, California and Pacific Northwest Forests)* in the Peterson series. John is a Fellow in the American Ornithologists Union and has served as president of the Association of Field Ornithologists and Wilson Ornithological Society. He is currently a member of the board of directors of the American Birding Association.

43. *Share Your Passion: Born-Again Birder*
by Peter Stangel

SHARING YOUR PASSION is good for birds, birding, and conservation.

I was "born again" as a birder in the spring of 1992. It changed my life, and I'm going to witness to you right now. Can you say "Amen"?

It happened on Asilomar, on California's Monterey Peninsula, where I was attending a bird-conservation conference. After a morning of spirited discussion, I joined a female friend for a walk to the coast to look at shore birds.

We made our way to a small bluff overlooking the peninsula's sprawling beach, which was peppered with birds. Dozens of walkers, bikers, in-line skaters, and others patrolled the paved walkway that hugged the edge of the precipice. My friend, eyeing some birds along the water's edge, extended the legs of her tripod, confidently placing her spotting scope square in the middle of the walkway.

Horrified that we might draw attention to ourselves as birders, I grabbed the scope and slid back into the nearby brush, hoping no one would see us. Just as quickly, my friend put the scope back on the pavement. I shot a glance

down the walkway, spied an older couple power-walking toward us, and counted down the number of seconds until my ultimate embarrassment.

My fears were quickly realized. "Hey," my friend shouted to the couple. "Why don't you take a look at these birds through my spotting scope?" The couple hesitated, intrigued, more curious than startled. As Californians, they were clearly accustomed to atypical behavior. The man cautiously approached the eyepiece and stared through it for several seconds. He backed away, allowing his companion a peek. "Why do those birds have such long bills?" he quizzed my friend.

I was still doing my best to imitate one of the nearby Monterey pines, so my friend took over. "They're dowitchers," she said, "probably Long-billed. They use their bills to probe into the sand in search of invertebrates, their primary food." The brief discourse on dowitcher ecology concluded when the gentleman noted that, although he had lived on the peninsula for more than a dozen years and had seen many birds on the beach, he never knew what they were. "Thank you," he said, collecting his mate and resuming his stroll. His companion, who never spoke, smiled and nodded her agreement.

No one escaped my friend's invitation that sunny afternoon. No one refused her offer. No one laughed at her, and almost everyone had something positive to say. Some commented on the birds, some on the spotting scope. Several shared stories about an aunt or friend who loved to watch or feed birds. Emboldened by my friend's success, I gradually emerged from the shrubbery and began to participate. Sharing birds with these strangers made me feel good about being a birder.

Later, as I reflected on my experience, three things stuck in my mind. First, I had fun. Second, all with whom we shared the birds enjoyed the experience. Third, no one poked fun at us! My eyes were opened that glorious day, and my life was changed. Can you say "Amen"? Why had I not been born again as a birding evangelist until the age of thirty-something? A quick recall of my youth provided the likely answer. As a young birder, especially as a teenager, I had suffered some embarrassing experiences, mostly at the hands of my peers. "Nature boy," they accused when they caught a glimpse of me with my binoculars.

Their comments stung, and I retreated, both emotionally and physically. I hid my birding behavior, carefully avoiding others while in the field. I slipped my binoculars inside my jacket when people approached and jammed bird books deep inside my pockets. I never mentioned what I saw. I became a closet birder.

The experience at Asilomar made me realize, however, that this retreat robbed me of the pleasure of sharing birds with others. It was also detrimental to birds and bird conservation. Who knows how many people I might have turned on to birds and conservation during my lost years?

I left Asilomar with renewed spirit and boldly went where all birders should go — right to the general public. No one is safe today when I am around. I seek out passersby and implore them to borrow my binoculars or look through my scope to enjoy a bird. I go out of my way to let hotel clerks know that I'm in town to bird, and I share my day's tally with them. I interrupt tennis matches to point out Cooper's Hawks as they glide by. I now wear my binoculars outside my jacket as a badge of pride and an invitation to others to ask what they are for. I'm a birder and proud of it!

Sharing my enthusiasm for birds has provided some very rewarding and unexpected experiences. A few winters ago, for example, a small group of us were gawking at two adult Bald Eagles perched on the frozen Potomac River in Washington, D.C., eating fish trapped in the ice. Our trance was broken by a tour bus that pulled up behind us and disgorged a dozen young adults. Based on their unique combinations of leather, Lycra, and denim, they were clearly city kids and, by dialect, probably from New York City. I turned to my colleagues, wondering if we should extend an invitation. Without my asking, they nodded their agreement. I bit the bullet. "Hey! You guys want to see some neat birds?"

They came our way, laughing nervously. One by one, they peered through the spotting scope. "Cool!" "Awesome!" "Way!" They were clearly impressed, and they asked a lot of questions. The last to come forward was a young man. The others deferred to him, so I assumed he was their leader. It took him several seconds to get comfortable with the scope, and he looked for quite a while. Finally, he pulled back and looked me right in the eye. He motioned for me to come toward him. Oh, great, I thought, I show him these cool birds and now he's going to mug me! Summoning my suburban courage, I walked toward him.

He leaned toward me. "Do you know what my favorite bird is?" he asked. Surprised but still wary, I winced. "No, I don't." He reached down with both hands and yanked up his T-shirt, revealing a chest-wide tattoo of a flying Bald Eagle. "Eagles are my favorite birds," he confided. Speechless, I could only nod in agreement and thank my lucky stars. Eagles brought the two of us together in a way that not much else could have.

Sharing my fervor for birds is now my favorite part of birding. I'd much rather share local birds with a bunch of beginners than chase after some phone-tree rarity with other fanatics. I rarely bird by myself now — it's just not as much fun if I can't share the birds with someone else.

In addition to enhancing my birding experience, I also feel that I'm making a contribution to bird conservation. I embellish my commentary with conservation tips — keep your cat inside, buy a Duck Stamp, bird-proof your windows. Maybe, just maybe, some of the people with whom I share my passion will get hooked themselves. That can only mean good things for birds and their future.

Please don't enjoy my experience vicariously. Come out of the closet. Be born again. Birds are fantastic, and not to share them is to do yourself, humanity, and birds a tremendous injustice. Yes, it takes a little courage. But when you see the enthusiasm with which people respond, it will all be worth it. Take a chance. Share your passion for birds. You won't be disappointed. Amen!

———

Peter Stangel's career in conservation began when he provided backyard bird-feeding tips to his second-grade class in elementary school. After receiving a Ph.D. in ecology from the University of Georgia, he joined the National Fish and Wildlife Foundation (www.nfwf.org), where he coordinates bird and regional conservation efforts in the South.

44. *Let Birds Help You Escape to Paradise*
by Stephen Shunk

Paradise is not just a tropical beach. It can be found in the roar of a city, in the silence of falling snow, during the tedium of a commute, and even in the midst of a natural disaster.

⌄ ⌄ ⌄

THE LIGHT RAIL ROLLED up First Street, flanked by a row of buses waiting for commuters to make their transfers. The city's heartbeat echoed through the tunnels of tall buildings. San Jose is a clean city, its downtown streets lined with benches and planters and pedestrian corridors as wide as the streets themselves. Breaking the distant horizon, the warm spring sun skimmed across the urban canopy. The jungle below remained cool and shaded at street level.

As the railcar departed, I walked behind, and the din of downtown faded. Falling from thirty stories above, a familiar chatter broke the relative silence. A distinctive *jeee, jee, jee, jee, jee, jee, jee,* descending in pitch and seemingly in stereo, caught my ear, and I turned my eyes to the sky.

Overhead, lit like ornaments in the rising sun, a flock of White-throated Swifts zigged and zagged above the buildings. As quickly as they appeared, they were gone, but this image remained with me until I fell asleep that night.

Even in the city, birds can help us tap our innate connection to wildness. A flock of tiny swifts, weighing all of an ounce and a half each, has the power to raise our spirits above the maze of concrete and steel that surrounds us.

❧ ❧ ❧

Aching for some exercise, we tossed our skis in the car and headed up the mountain. The snow flurries on the flats changed to a steady dump at the pass. We resisted the urge to turn back and proceeded to the trailhead. Two feet of new, wet snow awaited us, a trudge at best. After scaling the berm at the edge of the parking lot, we found a recently set path, relieved that someone else had broken trail.

The parking lot was bereft of birds. Even the resident Gray Jays declined to greet us in the heavily falling snow. I needed some birds to keep me motivated. Every ten minutes or so, I stopped and uttered a few pygmy-owl toots, hoping for a nuthatch or kinglet. Anything. After thirty minutes of slow progress and no birds, we lacked the desire to continue. Just before turning around, I heard a familiar purposeful tapping a short distance off in the burned forest. We left the trail and set a bead for that sound. Not thirty yards away, we found a female Three-toed Woodpecker excavating a roost cavity near the top of a fifteen-foot snag. She sought shelter from the falling snow. Her cavity was already head-deep, and we watched in awe as the tiny chips flew.

The birds are there, somewhere. Finding them might require some work, but they are there. They can ameliorate frustration or bring light to a dark forest on a snowy winter's day.

❧ ❧ ❧

I dreaded crossing the bridge during morning rush hour. As I passed through the last tunnel, I saw the Golden Gate before me, so close, yet so far away. The traffic slowed, and I searched the radio for some kind of aural distraction. Even the fog bank approaching from the ocean side of the bridge moved faster than our tiny vehicles lining the pavement of this mammoth structure.

I finally made it onto the bridge, relieved that the traffic would soon split into two slightly more fluid arteries on the other side. The music wasn't doing the trick, and my momentary relief alternated with anxiety. I could have left an hour later and cruised into the city with ease. What was my rush? While I chastised myself for the poor planning, a silver streak arose from the bay side of the bridge and bolted across my hood. Before I could take my next breath, it was gone, but there was no mistaking the brilliant impression now embossed in the airspace before my windshield. I had heard that a pair of Peregrine Falcons lived under the bridge, but now I had seen for myself.

Birds have power. Not just the power of the Peregrine to subdue its prey but the power to transform arduous routine into spontaneous escape. Birds can help us avoid tedium, carrying us to a place far away and sometimes through seemingly impenetrable barriers.

∨ ∨ ∨

I arrived at work on time, which was a little earlier than usual. I walked onto the sales floor and greeted my coworkers as I had done dozens of times before. I made eye contact with my friend Steve, and he nodded his head in acknowledgment of the mundane evening ahead. Before I could nod back, our line of sight was interrupted. The floor dropped, and the building shook. A deep booming sound drowned all others. We all knew what was happening; it had happened dozens of times before. But this time, it was different. This felt like "the big one."

The building lost power, and shoppers and staff packed into every available doorjamb. The movement of the rafters snapped off an overhead sprinkler, setting off the whole system and adding confusion to the chaos. After what seemed like forever, everyone moved toward the nearest exit, most at least fearful, others quite panicked. I reached the front door and set foot in the foyer, then on the asphalt, and I looked to the sky. The first thing I saw was a gull, flying effortlessly through the parking lot and alighting on a lamppost, just as it had done dozens of times before. It was unfazed by this stretching of the Earth's crust. For a moment, I escaped with the gull to a familiar world. One filled with birdsong and the breeze through the trees, one where I am surrounded by nature. I realized that I could visit that place anywhere, anytime, guided by the wings of a single bird.

The world is what we make of it. It can be mediocre, frustrating, or even exasperating. Or not. As long as there are birds, there will be an alternate world inviting us to immerse ourselves in its magic and vigor, and any time we lose sight of it, we need only look to the birds, who are always there to guide us to this place called Paradise.

———————

STEPHEN SHUNK is a freelance writer, nature-based tourism consultant, and field ornithologist living in the shadow of central Oregon's East Cascade Mountains. Through his company, Paradise Birding, Steve also leads birding tours throughout the western United States. He is currently writing the *Peterson Reference Guide to Woodpeckers of North America*.

45. *Slow Down and See More Birds:*
The Rule of Sandwiches
by John Acorn

LIFE IS SO HECTIC these days. Modern society forces us to rush. It's called "time management," or "cost-benefit analysis." Time is money, and money matters. It is no wonder, then, that birding is such a popular escape from these misguided priorities. And it's no wonder that most birders approach their time in the field in exactly the same silly way.

You know what I mean, right? Haven't you heard birders talk about the need to "work" a trail, "maximize their species list," or "cover as much ground as possible"? Haven't you noticed how the frenzied quest for bird sightings is precisely reminiscent of the frenzied quest for wealth, power, and prestige in the working world?

Well, I have some good news for you. Good birders don't rush frantically about like wild dogs coursing over a field in search of the scent of prey. Instead, good birders are like mountain lions — they lie in wait (in a likely spot, of course) and wait for their quarry to come to them.

Take my friend Kari, for example. He loves to lie on the

ground, on his back, smoking a cigar and looking straight up into the sky, in search of birds overhead, at least when the smoke plume isn't a problem. He impressed us all when he started seeing Pacific Loons and other rare water birds over his suburban front yard in Edmonton, but when he started finding Smith's Longspurs at Beaverhill Lake, our best local birding spot, we were amazed. You see, none of us had ever seen a Smith's Longspur here, even though we knew they probably came through on migration. The trick is to recognize them from below as they fly overhead.

For me, the realization that slow and easy works wonders came when I took up fly-fishing. As I ever so slowly waded my way up narrow trout streams, inching toward rising fish, I started to see — Soras! Before that, I only heard Soras, or caught fleeting glimpses, but now I see them all the time.

Big deal, you say? Well, perhaps you can relate to what happened to my friend Jack. Jack is an entomologist, and not long ago he found himself on a day trip with two birding friends, searching for Mountain Plovers on a deserted patch of southern Canadian prairie. The two birders grabbed their lunch and their binoculars and set off hiking across the prairie to find the plovers. Jack stayed near the car, set up his lawn chair, and watched digger wasps bury paralyzed caterpillars in the sand. Late in the day, the two birders returned, exhausted and disappointed to have missed the bird. That's when Jack asked them, "Hey, guys, what kind of bird looks a lot like a Killdeer but is just plain brown? There was one right here for most of the day — it just flew away when you came over the hill . . ."

I used to host a television show about birding called *Twits and Pishers*. If you've ever been on television outdoors, you know what it's like. You get to the spot, you set up the camera, and then you wait. Sometimes you wait for a plane or a boat to go by, so it doesn't mess up your soundtrack. Sometimes you wait for clouds to pass. Sometimes you wait for some guy to quit using his chain saw or jackhammer. Sometimes you wait for noisy birders to move on down the trail. But most of the time, you just wait, and that's when the great birds start to show up.

This seemed to work best for us in the tropics. At the Asa Wright Nature Centre in Trinidad, our production crew was surrounded by hotshot birders, both American and British, and their groups were always off hiking the trails or hiring guides to take them in search of more species elsewhere on the island. We, by contrast, moved slowly and sat around a lot. And at the end of the day, the "Competitive Power Birders" (that's what Larry the soundman called them) were jealous of us. "You saw *what*?" they would exclaim, and we would show them the footage of the Ornate Hawk-Eagle on its nest, the Barred Antshrike eating the

Copper-rumped Hummingbird, and the King Vulture soaring over the main building at the center.

On another television show, we discussed this phenomenon in detail, and my raptor biologist–guest Gordon Court had a name for it: the rule of sandwiches. In other words, the rare bird shows up not while you are looking for it but the minute you put down your binoculars and pick up your lunch.

You may have heard of the Big Sit, a birding event in which you force yourself to stay within a fifteen-foot circle for twenty-four hours and count birds. Great idea, I say, but even for me twenty-four hours is a bit like overkill. Why do we always do things to excess or not at all? I'd like to introduce the concept of the Little Sit, a technique you can use almost anywhere, anytime. It may not always pay off, but when it does, it feels great.

And then there's "still walking," the favorite technique of my birding buddy Brian. Brian likes to make his way to a productive area, walking slowly, and then start walking really, *really* slowly, so slowly that you can barely see him move, as in tai chi. In fact, it takes forever for Brian to bring his binoculars to his eyes once he spies a good bird. Last spring, Brian was demonstrating this technique for our somewhat impatient but still lovable friend Rose. A warbler chipped in a willow to their right, but it was gone by the time Brian completed the turn toward it.

"The bird flew away, Brian!" snipped Rose.

"Not to worry," replied Brian, his lips barely moving. "It'll be back on fall migration."

———————

JOHN ACORN is a biologist, writer, broadcaster, and university lecturer living in Edmonton, Alberta. He is co-author of two Canadian bird field guides and frequently travels to speak at birding festivals and to watch birds.

46. *Go Birding with Kids*
by Alicia Craig

THE AVERAGE BIRDER WOULD probably be less than thrilled to take a child on a bird walk. Children typically are noisy, have short attention spans, and usually are not interested in trudging through the woods to find a bird — let alone stand there and study the bird while consulting a book to be sure the wing bars and eye-rings match the picture.

I, by contrast, really enjoy taking children out to watch birds. I have taken many children out bird watching, including my own child, children who visit the nature center where I volunteer, scouts, and various camp and school groups. I am often asked, "Why on earth do you like birding with kids so much?"

Well, the answer is simple — if at least one child out of the group I take birding is turned on by watching birds and starts to care about birds, then I feel good about being able to share the experience with a younger generation. It is really fun to watch kids get excited about the birds they see. Once a child figures out bird watching can be fun, it no longer feels like a boring activity she has been dragged out to participate in.

There are some tricks you can use if you decide to take a child or group of children birding. Once you find the children (contacting your local nature center, school, or scout group is a great way to find a group of kids to take birding), find a location you know will have some birds. I like to have a location that includes a pond or some sort of water source. If you are really stuck for places to go, setting up feeders beforehand can be helpful.

I usually start by quickly sharing a few pictures of some of the birds I expect to see on our walk. I also include a tape recording of the birds so the children will be able to hear some of the sounds the birds make. (I really like the IdentiFlyer — the sounds are not perfect, but they serve the purpose. Gadgets are great for kids, and using them seems to hold their attention a little longer.) I divide tasks among the group, asking one child to keep a list of what we see, one child to carry the IdentiFlyer, a few kids to carry the cards that go into the gadget, and another to carry the bird book. I typically don't worry about binoculars; however, I do usually take a spotting scope.

After I have introduced the kids to the sights and sounds of some of the birds they are most likely to see on our walk, I explain some of the rules about bird watching. I usually whisper these rules to the group. I whisper because the children tend to listen, and doing so gets across my point about being quiet. I let them know that the less we talk and the less noise we make, the more birds we are likely to see on our walk. I let kids know it is okay to point out a bird — just don't yell. I ask them to raise their hands and watch for me. If they stop and stand still, I will probably look at them to see what they are up to. So the rules are no talking, walk quietly, keep together, and share the bird book. Okay — off we go.

I start the bird walk by finding a spot to pish the birds. It is pretty easy to pish in some small birds so the kids can see them. I don't think I have ever led a walk when pishing didn't work, and it is really fun to see the kids' eyes light up as they wonder how on earth I did that. Every once in a while throughout the walk, I stop and pish and listen. I sometimes play the sounds from the IdentiFlyer (asking the various children to share their cards). I ask "Who has the chickadee?" or "Who has the screech-owl?" so they have to think about it and look for the bird I am requesting.

Our walk typically leads to a water source where I can set up the scope and have them look through the lens to see if they can find the duck (which I have cleverly spotted). Having kids look through binoculars can be problematic at first — they tend to play with the binoculars and sometimes have trouble spotting the birds through those tiny lenses. Once I have taken a group out several times, or if the group has fewer than five kids, I sometimes have the kids use binoculars. But in most cases I stick with the spotting scope.

I try to point out the best way to identify a bird by shape, size, and comparison with birds the kids may easily recognize, such as a robin, sparrow, or crow. I always mark ahead of time the field guide pages with the birds we are likely to see so I don't have to fumble through the book. I also ask the designated book-carrying kids to look up birds for me. If a child sees a bird and doesn't know what it is, I ask these questions: What size is it — bigger than a sparrow, the size of a robin, or bigger than a crow? What color is the bird? What else about the bird do you notice? (I suggest things such as a really small or large bill and small or large legs and feet.)

It sometimes takes a while to work through all the clues, and I almost never just tell them the identity of a bird. The caretaker of the list reports back to the group at the end of our trip about the birds we have seen. I like to discuss anything special about the birds we see. I try to do this in the field while we are looking at the bird, but in many cases, I wait until we return to the nature center or classroom. I usually end my bird walk with a brief discussion about what kids can do to help protect birds (keep their cats indoors, don't litter or cause pollution, create a habitat at home or at school for birds, and volunteer at a local nature center).

I have always had fun on my bird-watching trips with children. In fact I have almost more fun with kids than I do with adults. I encourage every bird watcher to take children bird watching. It can be fun for you and fun for the kids!

———

ALICIA CRAIG is director of the Bird Conservation Alliance for American Bird Conservancy. She has worked as a naturalist in Florida and for a national bird-feeding retail organization. Craig serves on the American Ornithologists' Union Committee on Conservation as well as on several other ornithology boards and councils. She has appeared on television programs such as PBS's *Birdwatch*. She lectures and presents workshops to all age groups on bird identification, conservation issues, and habitat creation. Craig lives with her daughter in Indianapolis.

47. *Introduce Children to Birds*

by Laura Erickson

WHAT IS IT ABOUT birds that fascinates children? Humans' eyes and ears are attracted to color, sound, and movement. Brilliant plumage, lovely songs, and graceful flight can grab anyone's attention, avian or human. Birds are much tinier than humans, making them seem vulnerable to even the smallest child, yet they hammer holes into the hardest trees and weave the softest, most intricate nests. They're masters of air and water yet can hop and run on solid ground. Birds are also shape shifters. A robin's characteristic silhouette on the ground changes entirely when it takes wing. A floating duck isn't much different in shape from a waddling one, but when it opens its wings and launches into high-speed flight, it seems a different creature altogether.

We adults often assume that children need "accessible" books and give them simplified field guides. But a field guide with vibrant pictures and clear range maps is far more than a mere identification directory; it's an appealing invitation to learn more about birds. When I opened my first field guide at age twenty-three, I finally was able to identify the dancing Western Grebes I'd seen for many years on television ads for *Wild Kingdom*. Ever since I'd read *White Fang* in fifth grade, I was captivated by the word *ptarmigan* — White Fang's first hunting success was a brood of tasty ptarmigan chicks and their mother. Now I finally knew what they looked like. My new field guide also solved a mystery from my early childhood. One morning I'd looked out my bedroom window at my maple tree to see a rainbow of tiny birds splashed with brilliant yellows, deep blues, soft greens, bright orange, licorice black, and gleaming white, each different from the others. My mother told me they must be someone's escaped canaries, but they looked far too bright and animated. When, as an adult, I opened my field guide to the Wood Warblers, there they were, exactly as they'd been etched into my memory.

One of the best gifts an adult can give a child is a map of the world with a star pinpointing the child's home range. Most children have relatives living in other places. Put stars on those places, too. When you take a trip, trace your route on the map. Little by little, you'll give the child a far more vivid sense of the Earth and help put many important concepts of history and geography into a more meaningful context. When you take the child to a zoo, point out range maps for the animals and help the child understand that toucans, ostriches, and penguins all live as free as robins, cardinals, and Blue Jays somewhere on

Earth. Then the child won't reach college age still thinking, as I did, that "zoo animals" are just that.

Should you buy binoculars for children? Until a child is in at least third grade, I think not. You don't want to distract a kid from singing robins and quacking ducks by fiddling around with optics. Children's eyes are keener than ours, allowing them to see a surprising amount of detail. Small children do like to emulate adults, but rather than buying cheap plastic binoculars, which give a cloudy view even before they get scratched and knocked out of alignment, tape two toilet paper tubes together and fashion a neck strap from a long shoelace. Binoculars serve two functions. They not only magnify a view but also provide "tunnel vision" so that we can focus on one thing without side distractions. Cardboard-tube binoculars serve that function perfectly.

When a child graduates to real binoculars, start with 7- or 8-power magnification. These give a wider field of view than 10-power and provide more light at twilight and in the dark. Make sure that the binoculars are weatherproof and shockproof and that they have a rain guard — remind children to put the rain guard on the eyepieces before eating or drinking. Eyecups should be pushed in for eyeglass wearers and fully extended for those who don't wear glasses. Help children set the barrels for the distance between their eyes so they don't see blacked-out images.

Finally, when you introduce a child to binoculars, show how you keep your eyes on the object as you pull the binoculars up, and help the child practice this skill first on signs, trees, and other stationary objects.

When you take small children on bird walks, keep your eyes and heart open to what they are experiencing, not what you think they should be experiencing. Your heart may pound with excitement when you spot the first Kirtland's Warbler ever recorded in your state while the four-year-old at your side focuses on male cowbirds strutting around a female, opening their wings and bowing while making delightfully liquid squeaky sounds. You may thrill at a distant Eurasian Wigeon among migrating ducks while the child beside you is entranced by the way the head of a nearby Mallard glows as it changes from green to purple to green again.

If the birding bug is embedded in our DNA, it's apparently a somatic mutation, not something transmitted via our parents. Once in a while avid birders produce birding children, but more often than not, young birders are sparked by grandparents, teachers, and other nonparental adults. Quite a few of my students developed a lifelong interest in birds, but not one of my own three children has become a lister, though they are interested in and care about birds. I'm not sure whether I dragged them to one too many sewage ponds or whether they simply decided to carve out their own identities by having hobbies and interests separate from mine. I may believe deep in my bones that no one should go through life listlessly, but far more important than keeping bird lists is understanding and caring for the rich natural diversity and abundance of our planet. Share that with children, and you'll be giving them the world.

———

LAURA ERICKSON is host of the popular radio show *For the Birds* and serves as staff ornithologist for Binoculars .com. She also writes regularly for BirderBlog.com and is the author of *101 Ways to Help Birds, For the Birds: An Uncommon Guide,* and *Sharing the Wonder of Birds with Kids.* She lives in Duluth, Minnesota.

48. *Work at Becoming a Good Birder (Maybe Even a Great One)*
by Pete Dunne

Ever seen a really good birder in action? How about a great one? Birders who can pin the name Willow Flycatcher to some plain brownish *Empidonax before* it sneezes: *Fits'bew*. Birders who can identify raptors soaring two time zones away. All birders would like to be better birders, and it's not too much of a stretch to say that all birders, deep in their hearts, would like to be great birders.

Well, what's stopping you? Good birders (even great ones) are made, not born. You show me an accomplished field birder, and I'll show you a person who set his sights on becoming precisely that. Care to emulate him? Here's what you have to do.

1. GET BUSY BEING BUSY

You want to be a really good birder? Get busy. It's going to take a focused effort. It's going to require that you frame your objective. Anybody can go birding and increase her skills. But the best go birding with the express objective of learning their subject.

Will Russell, founder of WINGS Birding Tours, is on everybody's short list for title of Finest Field Birder in North America. I once asked him how he got so good. His four-word response, "I work at it," speaks volumes and offers two insights worth affirming. Note first that he said "work." *Work* means effort. Note, too, that Will framed his response in the present tense. Good birders are never static, never complacent, never good enough. They are constantly pushing their limits and thus increasing the level of their skills.

2. USE GOOD EQUIPMENT

Can you be a really good birder without owning quality optics? Yes. But it's going to make your task harder. You should know that the people who write and illustrate field guides use very good optics. Their descriptions and illustrations are predicated upon the images ferried to their brains along those quality-impregnated tubes. If you want to enjoy empathetic accord with your field guide, you should enter the game comparably equipped so that what you see in the field is what artists and authors illustrate and describe.

3. BIRD, BIRD, BIRD, BIRD, BIRD

To be a good birder, you have to bird a lot. How much is a lot? A lot is pretty nearly all the time. Being serious is called best intentions unless you combine it with lavish amounts of time in the field. The very best birders are in the field at every opportunity, and frankly, they are really never not birding.

4. BIRD WITH BETTER BIRDERS

Half a century ago, the difference between a beginning birder and an accomplished birder was, maybe, two or three years. Now it's closer to one or two decades. Birding's skill and knowledge base have grown exponentially. That's the bad news. The good news is that, unlike many human endeavors, which are motor-skill-driven (such as golf or platform diving), birding is information-driven, and information is easily shared and banked.

Going out with more experienced birders will help you with your identification skills because with mentors the uncertainty factor that dogs beginners is minimized. You'll learn tricks and shortcuts to difficult identifications. You'll get to know what puts the "good" in "good birder" and have a mark to shoot for, but . . .

5. GO BIRDING BY YOURSELF, TOO

One of the cardinal errors beginning birders make is not birding alone. They become habituated to going out with birders who are better than they are (such as the local expert at the nature center where they took their introductory bird course) and get into the lazy habit of letting the expert do the birding for them.

Uh-uh. Birding with good birders will shortcut the learning process. But then you have to apply and practice those skills yourself. If you let the local birding guru do the birding for you, you may get to see lots of birds, but your ability to identify birds on your own will almost certainly lag.

6. LEARN FROM YOUR MISTAKES

I love misidentifying birds. First, because I do it a lot. Second, because it presents me with my greatest opportunity for learning. Whenever you misidentify a bird, use the opportunity to try to understand why. Was it something about the way the bird was standing that reminded you of another bird? Was there something about a stage of molt that called to mind another, similar (even dissimilar) species?

The difference between accomplished birders and beginning birders is that accomplished birders have misidentified thousands of birds and beginning birders relatively few. But unless you use the advantage afforded by those misidentifications, you might succeed in becoming an experienced birder and still never be an accomplished one.

7. START YOUNG

This is a tough one (particularly if this window of opportunity has closed on you). How young is young? The very best birders I know started before high school, at an age when information is assimilated, processed quickly, and retained. Not all good birders had this advantage, and I can name half a dozen very accomplished birders who didn't start birding until middle age. But the fact remains that the very best birders — such as Kenn Kaufman, David Sibley, and Will Russell — all started young. Cheer up. They started out knowing less than you know now.

8. AND, LAST BUT NOT LEAST . . .

Have fun! The very best birders never lose the sense of fun — the joy they experience every time they watch birds. I guess it's possible to become a good birder by treating birding as if it's toil, but why would you want to? We humans tend to spend more time doing things we enjoy, and as pointed out earlier, one of the keys (perhaps *the* key) to becoming a good birder is to spend lots of time in the field.

So have fun. If you never succeed in becoming a great birder — or even a really good birder — at the very least you'll become a better birder. And what's wrong with that?

———————

PETE DUNNE is the author of eleven books, including *Pete Dunne's Essential Field Guide Companion, Pete Dunne on Bird Watching,* and *Hawks in Flight.* He is vice president of the New Jersey Audubon Society and director of its Cape May Bird Observatory, and has written columns and articles for virtually every birding magazine as well as for *The New York Times*.

49. *Cultivate Good Birding Practices*
by Jon L. Dunn

BIRDING, LIKE MOST fulfilling pursuits, requires skill and knowledge. Your level of expertise will depend on how diligently you cultivate the habits and practices outlined here.

1. LEARN DISTRIBUTION

Birders are always keen to learn the latest field marks to tell one species from another, but too often they don't learn distribution. The result is that they make numerous mistakes. Learning distribution means knowing the status of each species in your area. This includes the abundance level of each species, as well as regular arrival and departure dates and the outlying records. You should learn not only your own area but adjoining regions, too. Buy the best distribution books for your home area. This collection should include the appropriate state or provincial work for your area, but many excellent and more regional works also exist. Bruce Peterjohn's *The Birds of Ohio* is one of the best examples; one can quickly find the status of all species not only for that state as a whole but for any subregion of Ohio. *North American Birds,* a quarterly journal published presently by the American Birding Association, is another excellent way to learn distribution, not only for your region but for all of North America. As Louis Pasteur said long ago, "Chance favors only the prepared mind." Get informed.

2. LOOK AT THE BIRD IN THE FIELD, NOT IN THE BOOK

Way too often, birders fumble through their field guides while the bird is still within view. There is time enough to check the guide in the car or at home, long after the bird has flown. Savor the time to study the bird in the field, and in addition to carefully reviewing the field marks, study all aspects of the bird, including its behavior. The statement "It looked just like the picture in the book" is a sure sign that the observer spent more time looking at the book than at the bird!

3. KEEP FIELD NOTES WITH QUANTITIES

Always write a species list after an outing and write down actually counted or estimated numbers for each species. This will be an invaluable reference in the future, providing assistance in learning distribution. For a host of reasons, it can be useful for others as well. Don't trust your memory — write notes as soon as you finish birding a particular location. Be sure to include additional notes for the more unusual species or unusual numbers.

4. MAINTAIN YOUR INTEGRITY

If you find a rarity, look at it carefully and write notes about its appearance. Carry a camera, too, and try to document the bird with photos. You will be justifiably excited; after all, what could be more exciting for a birder? But calm down and reason with yourself. Remember that when you hear hoofbeats, they're more apt to be horses' than zebras'! Try to talk yourself out of it and work back through the field marks. If you are unsure or still believe you are correct, and after you have tried to get documentation (such as photos), contact others as soon as possible. Nothing creates skepticism quicker than the rarity that's not broadcast. Remember, too, that there is always the temptation, maybe even the pressure, to list something. It's hard to deny the reward we are seeking. Fight the temptation to be greedy — it's your reputation in the birding world that's at stake. And be ready to back down gracefully if you come to believe you might be wrong. This will increase your stature, not diminish it. Whether it be in birding or in anything else, the simple phrase

"I was wrong" is one that is so seldom heard, yet so refreshing.

5. LEARN FEATHER TOPOGRAPHY AND HOW TO WRITE A DESCRIPTION

Tedious as it might be, you need to know the parts of a bird. Some are easy and some are more complex, such as the stripes on the head or the configuration of the wing feathers. Knowing bird topography will help you to look for key field marks and write descriptions. When writing a description, organize it logically from the head down. Remember that others may read what you wrote and try to evaluate what you saw. If it's disorganized, that's harder to do.

6. USE MULTIPLE FIELD GUIDES

Most of us have a favorite, but that doesn't mean we should exclude others. Most guides have something valuable to say about each species. In addition to the field guides and a good distribution book, obtain a work that includes information about subspecies. Peter Pyle's *Identification Guide to North American Birds* (Part I) covers land birds. He's hard at work on Part II.

7. LEARN BEHAVIOR

In addition to learning the field marks, watch the behavior of the common species in your area. Often you can identify a species just by knowing its behavior. Even though the markings of a more unusual species may be unfamiliar, its behaviors may offer important clues about its identity.

8. CARRY A SCOPE

Birders often don't want to be encumbered by lugging a scope, but the better view a scope affords is worth the extra effort. Repeatedly relying on others' generosity with their scopes can get tiresome. When you carry your own, you can spend as long as you want observing a particular bird, and you have the opportunity to be generous by letting others look in *your* scope.

9. LEARN VOCALIZATIONS

Nearly all species can be recognized by their vocalizations, whether the primary song or the call notes and other contact notes, such as flight notes. Birders who start young and learn the calls are invariably the best birders out there. That means birders, and especially young birders, need to protect their ears from loud noises. Men in particular lose their high-frequency hearing as they age.

10. MINGLE WITH A FLOCK

For each group of birds, there is a strategy that is most effective for studying them. When studying shorebirds, for instance, find a location where you might be able to wade into the flock. Often shorebirds (especially the juveniles) will get totally accustomed to your presence and will come very close to you. Being surrounded by fifty or so individuals of a half-dozen species is a much better learning experience than peering through a scope at thousands of shorebirds of twenty species a quarter mile away.

11. LEARN FROM OTHERS

Most of us have mentors who offered sage advice in our early years as birders. Seek out a mentor. Be polite and listen. It's also a good idea to support your state or provincial ornithological organization. You can learn a lot from their publications and from the programs and field trips at their annual or semiannual conventions.

Jon L. Dunn has been chief consultant and editor for all five editions of the *National Geographic Field Guide to the Birds of North America*. With Kimball Garrett, he coauthored *Birds of Southern California, Status and Distribution*, and the *Peterson Field Guide to Warblers of North America*. He has been a long-serving member of the California Bird Records Committee and the American Birding Association Checklist Committee, and presently is a member of the American Ornithologists' Union Committee on Classification and Nomenclature. Dunn has been a leader for the popular birding tour company WINGS for nearly thirty years. He resides in Bishop, California.

50. *Recognize True Greatness*
by Richard K. Walton

Y ou know their names, although ironically most of the world is oblivious to their existence. They write books, lead international birding tours, paint with the talent of a Renaissance artist, speak at one birding convention after another, or perhaps write scholarly papers on evolutionary theory. These are the expert birders. And you have a hankering to join their ranks. Okay, fair enough — in America anyone can grow up to be the president.

This essay is not exactly a guide to becoming an expert birder; rather it deals with certain conditions, prerequisites if you will, necessary for ascending to the heights of the birding world. Yes, it's profiling. Use it at your own risk. No guarantees are implied. No refunds are available.

Although not considered a contact sport, birding has the potential to lay on a lifetime of bruises. True, these blows are largely to our egos and are seldom fatal, but they sting nonetheless. Still have aspirations to stand on the top step? Read on.

Those who choose to accept the full challenge of birding should be aware from the outset that the playing field is *not* level. As in any human endeavor, there are those born in the right place with the right stuff, and then there are the rest of us. Consider for a moment one stereotype of an expert birder. Born into a well-educated and wealthy family, our budding prima donna is coddled as a child and offered opportunities unavailable to most. Frequent visits to museums, family vacations to the tropics, nature camp each summer, and a place on Nantucket. If you are catching the distinct whiff of privilege, you are on the right track. This combination of native talent and opportunity confers on the lucky few a distinct advantage. Fortunately, many of these fine folks will end up in corporate boardrooms or playing polo. Unfortunately, a select few will become truly accomplished birders, leaving fewer spaces at the top for the rest of us. So if you don't know the verses to Camp Chewonki campfire songs, it's likely you don't fit this profile.

But there is still hope. Birders are a diverse lot, and the best of the best may even come from less fortunate bloodlines. Dysfunctional families have provided more than their fair share of expert birders. This is the story of success born out of misfortune. Here, too, genetic talent is a must, but in this case it is nurtured by adversity. A loner, the precocious child is left to his own devices, and somewhere along his aimless path he discovers birds. Unguided and unaware, the neophyte is not troubled by the prospect (or lack thereof) of a life devoted to birds. He is driven by an unquenchable thirst to know more about birds and an extraordinary energy born, ironically, from the void in his day-to-day existence. He appears out of the wilderness, with inappropriate binoculars slung about his neck and tattered field guide in hand, to take the birding world by surprise. If you haven't run away from home on several occasions, this is probably not the path for you.

So these are your best shots — privilege and adversity. A third profile presents a long shot. If you are still desperate for greatness but come from circumstances other than those just outlined, it's still possible (though not likely) to grab the ring. Once again (sigh), folks with average native skills need not apply. Yes, expert birders really do hear and see better than the rest of us. Their peripheral vision seems enhanced almost to the point of paranoia. While we are listening to the tanager thirty feet ahead, they are all over a warbler three hundred yards down the fence line. They can bring it, and they know it. But I digress. Among the world-class birders there are a select few who seem to have led normal, middle-class lives. One sure sign of genuine normality is the comfort you will feel in their presence. No edge, little defensiveness, and seldom a hint of their exceptional skills and knowledge. These rare folks seem self-satisfied and well centered. They will gladly lend a hand, answer a question, or just leave you alone. They may talk about sporting events, the Oscars, or flowering plants (in lieu of tertials, call notes, and allopatry). These birders take their children to the circus and may even introduce you to their parents.

With all due modesty, I must admit I have achieved a measure of success in the birding world. But greatness? Definitely not. For one thing, I was a late bloomer, not finding a passion for birding until my twenties. Expert birders typically develop their skills as children, when their synapses are still forming. And I just don't have the right attitude. The prospect of identifying a third-winter gull is anathema to me. You couldn't drag me to a Big Day — or even a Big Sit for that matter. Don't look for me on a small boat packed with birders desperate to add just one more pelagic species to their list.

So here's my pearl — my tip for the rest of us. First of all, know thyself. If you have the prerequisites for excellence, go for it. If not, be aware that birding can be approached from numerous angles. Art, literature, history, science, philosophy — all these disciplines and numerous others may be applied to birding. Find a niche that suits you, and it's likely you can become an expert in your own right. Work quietly and late at night until you are a master of your chosen turf. At a loss where to start? Here are a few fields just begging for an expert.

ART AND MUSIC

Sedges and grasses illustrated in John James Audubon's *Birds of America*
or
John James Audubon's favorite fiddle tunes

POETRY AND GOSSIP

The scurrilous poetry of Alexander Wilson, father of American ornithology
or
Illicit affairs attributed to Alexander Wilson, father of American ornithology

LITERATURE AND HISTORY

Ornithological references in the writings of Walt Whitman, William Faulkner, and Henry Miller
or
Birders in the White House: a history of birding in past and present administrations and its effects on foreign policy

So there you have it. While you will likely find more useful tips in other pages of this volume, none will serve you better than the following: Birding is both a passion and a pleasure. Exercise your passion, revel in the pleasure, and always bird with your tongue close by your cheek.

———————————

RICHARD K. WALTON is a teacher, writer, and naturalist with an interest in birds, butterflies, and dragonflies. He is coauthor, with Bob Lawson, of the Birding by Ear audios in the Peterson Field Guide series. Along with Greg Dodge, Walton runs Brownbag Productions and creates DVDs for naturalists. His research efforts focus on the Monarch Monitoring Project, which he founded in 1990 with Lincoln Brower.

INDEX

Index

10/07
598.07
WHITE